*For Beth —
One of "our very
own" — Appreciate your
service — and appreciate
you personally.
God bless you!*

Lengthening Legacy:
Eula Mae Henderson

by
Amelia (Millie) Bishop

Amelia Bishop

EAKIN PRESS ★ Austin, Texas

FIRST EDITION

Copyright © 1998
By Woman's Missionary Union of Texas

Published in the United States of America
By Eakin Press
A Division of Sunbelt Media, Inc., Austin, Texas
P.O. Box 90159
Austin, TX 78709
email: eakinpub@sig.net

ALL RIGHTS RESERVED.

ISBN 1-57168-261-9

Eula Mae Henderson

Contents

Foreword by Joy Fenner vii
I Am Grateful ix
1. *From the Sandpile to the Seminary* 1
2. *Classes, Corpus Christi, and a Call to Dallas* 9
3. *Looking, Listening, and Learning* 20
4. *Horizons Unlimited . . . at Home and Abroad* 35
5. *Diamond Jubilee . . . and Jubilant Days* 53
6. *On the Road, Onstage, Backstage* 70
7. *Outreach, Inreach . . . Labor, Levity* 87
8. *Changes, Choices . . . and Missions Firsthand* 102
9. *Shadows, Sunshine . . . Remembrances, Retirement* 120
10. *Journey's End . . . and a Lengthening Legacy* 140
    Endnotes 155
    Bibliography 161

Foreword

Eula Mae Henderson touched my life . . . and made a difference. This book is filled with glimpses of individuals in whom she saw potential and gave opportunities to develop. Countless others could be added, for she was a missions mentor to many.

She modeled excellence. A presentation of one minute or one hour. Writing a brief article or a book. Holding a poster or giving a major message. Being responsible for the lights and sound backstage in order for those onstage to be most effective. Eula Mae felt all should be done with excellence.

Lengthening Legacy paints a portrait of one woman's leadership over a 34-year period of Texas Baptist life. She saw remarkable changes in society, in churches, and in denominations. And through it all, she believed Woman's Missionary Union to be a vehicle that could link a woman to God's divine purpose.

There was no question but that Millie Bishop should be the one to write this book. Longtime friend and co-worker of Eula Mae's, she blends her research and journalistic skills with a heart for missions. She was serving as president of Woman's Missionary Union of Texas at the time of Eula Mae's death.

In 1986 Woman's Missionary Union of Texas established the Eula Mae Henderson Memorial Scholarship for women in graduate theological study who have chosen a career in missions or missions education. In God's providence, the first recipient was Judi Lee Bishop, Eula Mae's namesake (You'll have to read the book to understand that!). Today those talented women serve in Texas, other states, and around the world. Any profits from the sale of this book will be added to the scholarship fund.

Indeed the legacy lengthens. The influence of Eula Mae's missions commitment encircles the globe, touches lives, and makes a difference of eternal dimension.

                              JOY PHILLIPS FENNER
                              Executive Director-Treasurer
                              Woman's Missionary Union of Texas

I Am Grateful . . .

. . . to God, for the privilege of having written this book.

. . . to Joy Fenner, and to Woman's Missionary Union of Texas for asking me to do it. It has been a blessed journey down memory lane, bringing to me—as the song goes—"memories that bless and burn."

. . . for wonderful friends like Erma Henderson Barnett, Eula Mae's sister, for sharing with me so much of her childhood and teenage years with Eula Mae . . . and for Dollie Culp and Frances Stroope, both of whom served as administrative assistants to Eula Mae at different times, for checking over the sequence of events.

I am also indebted to Linda Crouch and Waunice Newton for painstaking proofreading. And certainly I could not have done without Ed Eakin, Virginia Messer, and Susan Temple of Eakin Press.

I thank Wilma Reed who chairs the WMU of Texas Archives Committee for making herself so available and helping me find my way through the archives. My thanks go also to archivist Alan Lefever, formerly of Southwestern Seminary and now of Baptist General Convention of Texas, for his support and assistance. In addition, I am indebted to Ellen Brown and Kent Keeth of the Texas Collection at Baylor University who made available the oral biographies of former WMU presidents with whom Eula Mae served. And let me thank Noemi Cuevas

Jimenez, my "resident expert" in Hispanic WMU's earlier days.

Certainly I would want to mention Alma Hunt and Helen Fling—longtime leaders in WMU, SBC—for encouraging me in the writing. And then, when computer problems made me wonder if I should do the whole thing by hand, there came my friend Brenda Baker, my computer guru!

May I thank also the many of you who responded when we sent the Eula Mae Henderson Questionnaires to friends and former staffers. Your input was invaluable.

Lengthening Legacy is not a history of WMU of Texas. That has been done three times since its beginning. But rather, this is the story of one woman whose life impacted WMU and who, in turn, was impacted by it.

AMELIA BISHOP

Dedication

This book is dedicated
to those whom Eula Mae called
"our wonderful Texas women."
She loved you.
And, as your letters have told me,
you loved her.
This is her story.
It is also yours.

1

From the Sandpile to the Seminary

"Let's just try and see how far we can get."

She was small for her age, and slender. She had dark curly hair and, just now, her large brown eyes were filled with concern. Church was the highlight of her week, and with the rain pelting down and the unpaved roads muddy, she heard her father say that they might not be able to go to church today. She knew he wanted to go as much as she—as did her mother and sister. And so she looked up at him and asked, "Couldn't we just try . . . and see how far we can get?"[1]

Of course, they did. And they got to church. That bit of philosophy, expressed with childlike faith, became part and parcel of the bedrock beliefs of Eula Mae Henderson, who served Woman's Missionary Union of Texas from 1946 through 1980. Elected in 1946 as Young People's Secretary, she became Executive Secretary-Treasurer (later Executive Director-Treasurer) in 1947 and held that position through 1980.

Eula Mae was born in Oklahoma City, Oklahoma, on August 8, 1915, to Rex and Alice Henderson, described as "wonderful Christian parents." She was an unusual child from the beginning, watching everything, crying little. She liked everyone. At church meetings, where she spent much of her time, she was the baby passed from person to person. When she began to walk, she was easily handled, Alice Henderson reported, because she seemed to be afraid of cats, baby chickens, and anything soft and fuzzy. "I don't know where this came from," Alice said on one occasion, "but I did learn that if I put something soft—like fuzzy cotton—around the edge of a table, Eula Mae would never touch it."[2]

Her father was employed at the Oklahoma Sash and Door Company; Alice (called "Mama" or "Al") was a homemaker and an excellent cook. They had been married six years and were delighted when Eula Mae was born. Three years later her sister, Erma, arrived.

"I don't remember much about the family home of my earliest years," Eula Mae recalled later. "As I remember, it was a four-room frame house and to this day I have a very warm feeling about it. It had a sandpile in the backyard and my sister and I spent many hours playing there. I also remember how special Christmas was. We had gone to church one Christmas Eve and it snowed. When we returned home, there were giant steps leading up to the house and my parents said Santa Claus must have been here. Sure enough, in the front room were two large, lovely dolls, one for Erma, and one for me. Looking back, I'm not sure how my folks worked all that out, but I do remember how excited Erma and I were."[3]

A little later, the family moved about a block away to what they called "the new house." It had a big living room, dining room, two bedrooms, kitchen, and a screened-in back porch. Mama sat there many hours shelling peas while the girls played jacks or embroidered. Alice also made the girls' dresses—replete with blue ruffles for Eula Mae, and pink for Erma.

The family car was an older model Ford. Rex left it at home and rode to work each day with a neighbor. Alice, the only woman in the neighborhood who could drive, was thus available to take mothers and small children to the doctor when the need arose, or to run other essential errands.

LONG, LONG AGO—Eula Mae (right) and her sister, Erma, pose in their "Sunday best" at the ages of six and three, respectively. At this point, the family lived in Oklahoma City.

THIS I REMEMBER: One of my earliest recollections of Eula Mae involves those times when I stood by the window, watching for her to come home from school, trudging down the road.

I knew her arrival meant two things: we would get a snack, and my sister would read to me.

You see, Mama made pie every day because Daddy did not think he had eaten at night unless he had pie, so many times our after-school snack consisted of pie dough with cinnamon and brown sugar, heated until it bubbled.

We would eat it, and then Eula Mae would read to me. She not only taught me to read, but also how to count, and how to play games like jacks. In fact, she taught me many things, and some of it didn't come out of books.

My sister was a significant part of my childhood. I am grateful.

—Erma Henderson Barnett

Eula Mae remembered walking eight or ten blocks to school. "I liked school," she said, "and I was always ready for it to start." She was a good student, skipping the fourth grade, and coming home each day to take her baby sister in her lap and "teach her" all she had learned that day. Those were choice family times.

At the age of nine, Eula Mae became a Christian. She had been attending Sunday School and church as long as she could

TIME FOR CHURCH—*Mrs. Henderson and her daughters, Eula Mae (center) and Erma rest a moment on the running board of the car while Dad finishes a last chore before departing for Sunday School. Sundays were special days in the life of the family.*

remember, as well as the missions organizations and BYPU—Baptist Young People's Union. "My conversion came during a revival in our church, Capitol Hill Baptist," she recalled, "and the evangelist was E. A. Petroff. I think I was impressed by the things he said, because I recall seeking out my mother one Wednesday afternoon while she was out in the back milking our cow. This was before we moved to the farm, but we did have a cow. I told mother how I felt, and she encouraged me to go forward that night. I did. I remember that when I walked down that aisle, there seemed to be something that connected my heart to the cross. As a child, I didn't understand all the theology involved. I just knew something connected me to Jesus and that cross, and I am grateful for the memory. I was baptized shortly after that."[4]

The family then moved to a farm near Luther, Oklahoma. The town had no Baptist church, and the family attended first the Methodist Church, and then the Christian Church. Mr. Henderson served as Sunday School superintendent; Mrs. Henderson taught a young people's Sunday School class. Eula Mae, who had been taking piano lessons since the age of nine, sometimes played the piano for church services. Music had become important in her life. She loved to open the hymnal, start at the beginning, and play through the hymnal as long as time permitted.

The church afforded some wonderful opportunities for the entire family.

Later, the Hendersons and other Baptists in the community decided they needed a Baptist church and invited friends from Oklahoma City to come and help them stage a brush arbor revival. The group came and as Eula Mae's sister, Erma, recalled, "Usually they ate dinner with us. I remember Mama would sometimes fix six pies for one evening to be sure she had enough."

The revival went well and the Luther Baptist Church was organized with the Hendersons as charter members. Eula Mae was regular in attendance and sometimes went several years without missing a Sunday. She played the piano, gave her testimony from time to time, and enjoyed the young people's fellowships. "Mostly, we ran around in groups," Erma noted. "Of course both boys and girls were involved, and Eula Mae particularly liked boys with brown curly hair."

The school the sisters attended was consolidated and included students of various age levels. The school bus they rode each day was crowded, and they were among the last to board. Because both were small and slender, they usually ended up sitting on the laps of the older young people.

Eula Mae sometimes spoke of a teacher named E. E. Cox, who had a decided influence on this stage of her life. His teaching ability and his encouragement were both meaningful to her. He taught math and one of his regular exercises was to send the students to the blackboard to do rapid calculations. "He would call out a long string such as 'Take nine, multiply by nine, add one, and divide by five. Now who has the answer?'" After several days of this, he would then challenge the students to do the problem in their heads. Eula Mae accepted the challenge and excelled. Math and English were favorite subjects; other interests included music and debate. She graduated as valedictorian of her class of 30 at the age of 16.

During her elementary and high school days she was

asked, as many are, "What do you want to be when you grow up?" Her first thought had been to be a school teacher; later, she thought about being a church secretary. "I really didn't think about becoming a denominational worker; I knew very little about Baptist life beyond the local church. That came later." Indeed it did.

After Eula Mae's high school years, it was decision time for the Hendersons. Her parents wanted to send her to college, but it was during the Depression and they could not. Hills Business College in Oklahoma City was the answer. She moved to Oklahoma City, rented a room with family friends, and started business courses. During this period, she worked part-time for a men's clothing firm. Upon graduation, she went to work for Myers Motor Company.

Meanwhile, the Hendersons had moved back to Oklahoma City. Their new home was near the Kelham Avenue Baptist Church, which they promptly joined. Eula Mae referred to this church as "one of three churches of significance during my growing-up years." She particularly remembered the fellowships. "You know, boys and girls were together, and it was more fun that way." She had set an ongoing program of study courses for herself and remembers a particular occasion when the Southern Baptist Convention met in Oklahoma City.

"I was in YWA—Young Woman's Auxiliary—and we had a small part on the program. While there, I heard for the first time Baker James Cauthen, later the head of the Foreign Mission Board of the Southern Baptist Convention. At that time, Dr. Cauthen was professor of Evangelism and Missions at Southwestern Baptist Theological Seminary, and he and his wife were leaving to be missionaries in China. I cannot remember his exact words, but the Lord used that occasion to help me understand that people could participate in missions in many ways. Later that summer, I made a commitment to the Lord on a Sunday morning in my church that I would be willing to serve Him in a special way. I didn't know what it was—my opportunities for knowing were still rather limited—but I was willing. I didn't feel called to be a missionary, although by this time I had heard wonderful people like Lucy Smith and Rosalee Mills Appleby, and both made impressions on me. I didn't like the idea of leaving my home and Myers Motor Company, but I felt like I was supposed to do something special, and I was willing."[6]

The five years at Myers had indeed been happy ones. "I loved the work," she recalled, "and I worked with some wonderful people. I was a bookkeeper and cashier, and I learned to operate the switchboard on the side." Leroy Dockum, a Baptist layman who worked there, was both helpful and encouraging. "He wanted me to improve myself, to set goals," she remembered. "I tried to move in that direction."[7]

And move she did. Reasoning that her decision would require special training, she considered the WMU Training School in Louisville, Kentucky. However, after talking with Mrs. Berta Spooner, Executive Secretary of Oklahoma WMU, Eula Mae decided on Southwestern Baptist Theological Seminary in Fort Worth, Texas.

She moved to Fort Worth in the late summer of 1939 to enter Southwestern Seminary.

A new chapter in her life had begun.

2

Classes, Corpus Christi, and a Call to Dallas

"It's our attitude toward something that often determines how we feel about it and what we do about it."

The 24-year-old seminary student with the dark curly hair leaned forward in her chair, her brown eyes fixed on the professor. She did not want to miss anything he was saying. After these months in Fort Worth, she had come to know him personally, to respect him, and, as her understanding broadened, to consider him one of the "greats" among Southern Baptists.

He was T. B. Maston, and the class was Church Recreation. But, as is the pattern of outstanding professors, Dr. Maston used the class time not only to teach the subject matter, but also as a springboard for encouraging his students to think. "Recreation," he would say. "Exactly what is it? We call baseball recreation, but is it really recreation to the man who earns his living that way? And the same could be said for professional athletes in any sport. Think about it. What makes the difference? I think you'll find it's the way you approach it, your attitude toward it."[1]

Eula Mae did think about it. In fact, her mind kept return-

9

ing to it. In later life she said, "I can go back even today and remember what Dr. Maston said. It made a deep impression on me. Truly, it is our attitude toward things that often determines how we feel about them and what we do about them. That was just one of the great things Dr. Maston helped me to reason through, and I shall always be grateful."

Having arrived at Southwestern Baptist Theological Seminary in the fall of 1939, Eula Mae found school both challenging and exciting, although she missed her family. (During her three years in seminary, she wrote a penny postcard home every day to her parents.) At first she was somewhat undecided about which courses to take, feeling that the Lord had a special task for her. Not knowing what that was, she focused on basic required curriculum. She soon decided that her real abilities were not so much with piano—as much as she loved it—but in the area of religious education. This became her focus.

She lived in the Women's Building, which later became Barnard Hall. The fellowship—or "girlship" as the residents sometimes said—was great, and Eula Mae made lifelong friends during these three years. One of these was Oleta Snell, who later became a missionary to Chile.

"Eula Mae was a devoted friend from our days at Southwestern," said Oleta. "When I left Texas in 1943 to serve in Chile, she was the last person I saw waving at me in the airport, and the first person I saw when I came home in 1948. During my 32 years in Chile, she met me every time I came home, and saw me off every time I left.[2]

"Sometimes getting me to the airport was a close call, but Eula Mae always said, 'I believe we can do it!' One particular occasion stands out in memory. The car would not start and time was short. We just breathed a prayer and then Eula Mae said, 'I'll try something someone showed me.' She hopped out of the car, raised the hood, and with a pencil in her hand, 'operated' on the car. I have no idea what she did, but it started. That was typical of Eula Mae."

THIS I REMEMBER: One day when Eula Mae and I were in Seminary, Orville Rogers, a friend of ours, took me up for my first plane ride. I had fun seeing Southwestern by air. In fact, when we flew low over the campus, I could see a baseball game in progress.

On my return to the dorm, the dorm president handed me a note which instructed me to appear immediately before the dorm council because I had broken a rule—I had ridden alone with a man! Dismayed and frightened, I made my way down to the assigned room with visions of being severely reprimanded or even expelled. When I stepped into the room with downcast eyes, the girls all burst into laughter, Eula Mae included. She had been a part of the whole thing. It was all one big joke!
—Sue Nishikawa

Another close friend was Frances Osborne. "All of us who lived in the dorm had a feeling of family," Frances recalled. "Eula Mae was especially easy to relate to. She seemed to have an appreciation of each person's gifts and what that individual could do in the Lord's work. She was very much an encourager."[3]

One of the major influences in Eula Mae's life during this period came in the form of Floy Barnard, who served on the Religious Education faculty. Eula Mae enrolled in Church

12   Lengthening Legacy: Eula Mae Henderson

SEMINARY DAYS—Eula Mae looks into the camera—and into the future—as she comes to the end of her three years at Southwestern Baptist Theological Seminary. Upon graduation, she joined the staff of the Morgan Avenue Baptist Church in Corpus Christi, Texas.

Drama, which brought her into direct contact with "Miss B." Although Eula Mae seldom mentioned her drama experiences, her classmates recalled she had major roles in several productions including "The Challenge of the Cross" and "The Rock."

What Eula Mae did mention on several occasions was the assistance Floy Barnard gave her in making speeches, and one specific assignment that had far-reaching results.

Dr. Barnard was asked to lead a conference for primary Sunday School workers at a State Sunday School Convention to be held in Houston. "She could not go, and she recommended that I have that opportunity," Eula Mae reported later. "It was worked out, and suddenly I found that here I was, a seminary student, taking the place of someone like Floy Barnard, a leader in religious education. It was somewhat frightening, but I was grateful for her encouragement, for the confidence she placed in me."[4]

The meeting was held at Baptist Temple in Houston, and the sessions went well. One of the women whom Eula Mae met was Mrs. T. C. Jester, prominent in associational and state

Woman's Missionary Union work, who later chaired the committee seeking a new Young People's Secretary for Texas WMU. That was linkage, but it would be several years down the road.

A third professor who contributed a great deal to Eula Mae's ongoing education was W. L. Howse, also of the Religious Education faculty. A number of years later, recalling her seminary days, Eula Mae said, "I remember he drew the outline of a long log on the blackboard, and then he put a small circle on one part of it and told us it represented a knot on the log. He pointed out that if you stand up close to the log, right in front of the knot, then that's about all you see; that what you really need to do is step back so that you see the whole log. It's like that with the programs of the local church. You have Sunday School, Training Union, WMU, Brotherhood, Music—they're all important. Each one contributes a certain something to the church program. That's why it is essential that a church staffer stand back and see the whole picture."[5]

"What Dr. Howse said was so important," Eula Mae continued. "I have tried to remember it through the years and see the whole religious education program of a church, not just WMU. I have a strong conviction that each organization does make a contribution, not just to the church, but to the life of the individual as well."

The need to see the whole picture—to appreciate the contribution made by each of the basic church programs—was one concept that Eula Mae returned to again and again. She believed it; she taught it; she practiced it, as evidenced by her own work in her local church and by the testimony of co-workers who promoted the different areas of work.

Others who made an impression on Eula Mae during her seminary days included L. R. Scarborough, President of Southwestern Seminary when she entered. "You had only to be around him to know that he was a great man of God," she stated later. "His name then—and now—is synonymous with evangelism. I also had the privilege of knowing Dr. and Mrs. E. D. Head a little later. Dr. Head followed Dr. Scarborough as the President of Southwestern, and Mrs. Head was active in WMU."

During her second and third years at the seminary, Eula Mae was on work scholarship and assigned to the business office. At that time, Baptist work in Texas was divided into 17 districts, and districts into associations. Each seminary girl with a work scholarship was assigned to a district WMU, and the women of that district would send her small gifts, write her notes of encouragement, and remember her on her birthday and at graduation time. Eula Mae was assigned to district five, the Corpus Christi area. The WMU did not pay for her scholarship, but they "mothered her" during her seminary days and came to know her by correspondence. This would prove an interesting linkage when she came to the end of her seminary career.

Eula Mae's interest in missions, initiated perhaps, when she heard Baker James Cauthen and missionaries in earlier days, was awakened during her last year at seminary. She served as President of the Young Woman's Auxiliary, having been installed by Mrs. B. A. Copass, then President of Texas WMU. The YWA was made up of all the young women in the dormitory. Meetings, held on Saturday nights, were highlights for many of the members, and involved mission activity as well as mission study. Eula Mae was conscious of a growing interest in missions and missions organizations, spurred on also by missionary speakers who spoke on campus from time to time.

The days at Southwestern were good ones, and she did not realize how soon she would have opportunity to put into practice what she had learned. N. B. Moon, a pastor from Corpus Christi, came to the seminary seeking an educational secretary for his church, Morgan Avenue Baptist Church. The names of five students were given him and he interviewed each of them. While visiting a friend in the business office, he mentioned he was seeking a secretary and the friend unhesitatingly recommended Eula Mae Henderson. Reverend Moon interviewed her and, being impressed that she was the one, invited her to visit the church in Corpus Christi.

The beginning of the weekend visit was less than auspicious. In the words of Floyce (Mrs. N. B.) Moon, "We met Eula Mae's train on a sultry Saturday afternoon. N. B. introduced me to an attractive, somewhat shy young brunette wearing a cotton dress. In those days, there was no wrinkle-free cotton, and she had spent a number of hours on the train. She was looking forward to changing her clothes but, much to her dismay, her luggage did not arrive with her. She was a good sport about it, and her hostess that night furnished her with the necessities. Fortunately, her suitcase did come the next morning. That worry was over!"[6]

Eula Mae's account of the weekend did not mention the luggage problem. "I went for the weekend," she reported. "They seemed to like me, and I knew I liked them. They were praying about it, and so was I. It all came together and I accepted their invitation to join the church staff."

Thus it was that in the late spring of 1942, following her graduation from Southwestern, she moved to Corpus Christi.

Morgan Avenue's paid staff at that time consisted of the pastor, Eula Mae, and the janitor. Although she was hired as an educational secretary, she also served as the pastor's secretary, helped with financial records, did education work, answered the phone, prepared the church bulletin, and worked with young people.

One of these, Eddie Jo Connell (Bazor) recalled both the long hours of serious discussion, as well as the fun times, with Eula Mae. "I remember how she helped me find my way during several crucial times in my life," she wrote. "She had a way of saying, 'Girl, I know we can. . .' And I remember also how we would ride the bus to get watermelon or ice cream, and then come back to her place and listen to an 'Advice to the Lovelorn' program on the radio and giggle at the answers."[7]

Other records list Eula Mae's activities in Vacation Bible School, summer camps, and associational and district meetings. Patsy Link (Deviney), a co-worker added to the staff, mentioned Eula Mae's expertise in the church visitation program. Many years later, EMH (as she was sometimes called by co-workers) would comment, "I have lived in Dallas for a long time, but I must say that those four and a half years in Corpus Christi were very, very special. I loved the people, and they loved me."

She recalled the mornings during revival services when the women's Sunday School classes would compete with each other for the high attendance record. "And," she added, "from noticing which women were there, I also knew how many we had in the nursery because I knew the children in each family. Later I had other responsibilities such as serving as Training Union director, which opened new doors. I became 'minister of announcements' in the Sunday night services, a role I became quite familiar with in the years that followed."

THIS I REMEMBER: Sometimes when I look at church bulletins, I think of Eula Mae. And rightly so!

When she and I worked together at Morgan Avenue Baptist Church, Corpus Christi, in the 1940s we put out the church bulletin on Fridays and Friday seemed to come around quite regularly! In those days, we certainly didn't have computers or even a Xerox machine, and so we cut the stencils ourselves. Then we ran them off on a hand-cranked mimeograph machine whose inking process left a lot to be desired. You had two choices: too much or too little!

Did Eula Mae get upset? No. She stayed happy and cheerful.

Did I? That's another story!
—*Patsy Link (Deviney)*

Being in Corpus Christi during the years of World War II also afforded a host of opportunities. A number of service men and women came to the church intermittently with varying needs. Sometimes the problem was loneliness, or the need for emotional support or some problem they felt they could not handle alone. Sometimes it was for help in finding a place to live. People seemed to be moving in or moving out constantly. "All these chances to help," Eula Mae said, "made you feel so close to the individuals involved, a part of their lives." And indeed she was.

It was the year after the war ended, in 1946, that an unexpected phone call closed one chapter of Eula Mae's life and opened another.

Floyce and N. B. Moon had gone to the annual meeting of the Baptist General Convention of Texas held that year in Mineral Wells. At that time, the position of Young People's Secretary on the Texas WMU staff was vacant and the Nominating Committee was seeking a replacement. On that committee were two women who had met or worked with Eula Mae in differing circumstances. One was Mrs. Harry Ward, a leader in district five WMU, who knew Eula Mae as a "District Five Scholarship Girl" and had later enlisted her to help in both associational and district work. The other was Mrs. T. C. Jester of Houston, who had met Eula Mae when she substituted for Floy Barnard at a Sunday School convention. The committee felt led to contact Eula Mae. First, however, they wanted more information and contacted Floyce Moon, who highly recommended the young church secretary. Hence, Eula Mae was called and invited to come to Mineral Wells for an interview.

"It was a bolt out of the blue to me," Eula Mae said later. "I never envisioned anything like that. I had no state-level experience; I had not been to a state convention; I didn't even know that Texas WMU had a position open. But interestingly enough, I had received a letter from my mother in Oklahoma City just a few days before this. She told me of a dream she had in which I had taken some kind of state position. Like myself, she knew nothing of what was going on in Texas WMU."[8]

Eula Mae told the women she would come for an interview.

"I already had a black crepe dress," she recalled, "so I

went to town and bought a new black hat. This was a time when women wore hats and I felt I just had to have a new one. Then I packed, got on the train and rode that night from Corpus Christi to Fort Worth. Mr. Lee Stephens met me at the station the next morning and took me to Mineral Wells. There I met with the 17 women serving as presidents of the districts in Texas who made up the Nominating Committee.

"I can't remember all their questions. They were kind, but thorough and tried to make the interview easy for me. I do recall that I wanted very much to be completely honest, and told them I didn't know a whole lot about WMU young people's work. Of course I knew about GA coronation services, but I had never done one personally. I would have much to learn, but I expressed my feeling that I could learn. I used a chocolate cake illustration. If you asked me to make a chocolate cake today, I'd have to say I don't know how. But I have the confidence that if I had a good recipe and the ingredients, I could learn; I could do it. I think I concluded by saying that if they thought I was the one, I would try. And so I was elected at that meeting. It was the fall of 1946. And a very special thing I remember about that occasion was that J. Howard Williams, who was then the Executive Secretary of the Baptist General Convention of Texas, sent me a note welcoming me to the Baptist Building."

On the way back to Corpus Christi, traveling in a car with five other women during the night hours, the full force of what had transpired hit her. "I could hardly imagine being in Corpus one day, and the next day telling the women in Mineral Wells that I would do state work," she remembered. "Surely I'm having a dream! Surely I didn't tell the women I'd do that!"

Back in Corpus Christi, she sought out Floyce Moon. The enormity of the change suddenly seemed overwhelming and her confidence was sagging. She began to doubt she could follow through on her commitment. "I can't do a job that big—I just can't," she said, expressing her deep down feelings. The pastor's wife listened, and then replied gently but with conviction, "No, you can't. Not in your own strength. But with the Lord's help, you can do it. You really can."[9]

And she did.

Chapter 2   19

Eula Mae finished her work at Morgan Avenue Baptist Church in late 1946 and moved to Dallas, to become Young People's Secretary for Woman's Missionary Union of Texas.

THIS I REMEMBER: During the time that Eula Mae served at Morgan Avenue Baptist Church, we had a teenager who was supposedly a part-time helper for our janitor. He was not particularly industrious, shall we say, and one day when the list was especially long, he showed up in the office and asked Eula Mae, "Miss Henderson, how do you spell 'resign'?"

Needless to say, from that time on, whenever things became difficult, someone would ask, "How do you spell 'resign'?"

—Floyce Moon

3

Looking, Listening, and Learning

"It is not enough to say we have more organizations, to claim we are doing better work. This we must do, but we must ever continue to reach out to provide early missionary education for young people."

The young woman with the dark curly hair and brown eyes stood at the Texas WMU Annual Meeting in Amarillo in 1947 to give her first report as Young People's Secretary. Her demeanor lent added earnestness to her words: "As we think about being laborers together with God, we realize that an honor has been conferred on us. With that honor comes a challenging responsibility; in my case, that of working with young people. Such a task has taken me into 47 associations in 16 districts this past year, traveling 21,107 miles. It is not enough to say we have more organizations. It is not even enough to claim we are doing better work." She went on to explain what she believed the ongoing challenge to be: "We must continue to reach out to influence others to provide early missionary education for young people."[1]

Thus it was that Eula Mae set forth and established in her first annual report what was to be one of the hallmarks of her three-plus decades in leadership of Texas WMU. She strove to broaden the scope of missions education both in quantity and in quality, and she was grateful when those efforts were crowned with success. Yet even in these instances, she felt the need to press forward, both in her work with the young people, and her work with the women. She quoted the oft-mentioned missiological statement, "The world is just one generation removed from spiritual darkness; if we believe in our mission, we cannot afford to slacken our pace."

When Eula Mae arrived at the WMU office at the beginning of 1947, the facilities were quite different from what they came to be in later years. The building which housed the offices was located at the corner of Ervay and Pacific Streets in downtown Dallas. The offices were quite small, and of course, this was before the days of air conditioning. On one occasion, Eula Mae described the big electric fans that sat on the floor, and smiled when she recalled the paper weights placed strategically on the desks to keep the letters from flying around. She shook her head, and added, "I still marvel at the amount of work done, the amount of materials mailed out, from that little space."

"At that time," she continued, "we worked five and a half days each week which was the schedule for the Baptist Building. We closed at noon on Saturday. Then came a time when just one person would be in each office on Saturday mornings—one in the Sunday School department, one in WMU, and so forth—and from that point, we moved to the five-day week."[2]

Rosalind (Mrs. Earl) Smyth had been elected President of Texas WMU at the Annual Meeting in Mineral Wells in 1946, the same session that Eula Mae had been elected. An experienced WMUer, Mrs. Smyth followed Crickett Keys Copass (Mrs. B. A.), who had held the position since 1931. Well-known to the women, Mrs. Smyth came to the office with impressive credentials as an effective organizer, a gracious parliamentarian, and a leader dedicated to personal soul-winning, stewardship, and leadership training.

Serving as Executive Secretary-Treasurer was Marie (Mrs. R. L.) Mathis, destined to highlight the pages of WMU history with distinction through several decades on state, national, and international levels. Her early work had begun on the local church and associational levels in east Texas. She then served on the state level as Benevolence Chairman, and in 1938 became Young People's Secretary, a position she held until 1945 when she became Executive Secretary-Treasurer.

As Eula Mae expressed it on several occasions, "Certainly no novice ever started with better instructors!"

Even the first day started well. Since a new Young People's Secretary had arrived, what would be the best way to start her off? Mrs. Mathis knew the answer. She assigned Eula Mae to work with Evelyn (Mrs. Bill) Beaird, an office secretary at the time. The two of them were to proofread the current copy of "Things We Should Know," a promotional piece of the era.

It was a good beginning. Eula Mae and Evelyn spent most of the day at the task, absorbed quite a bit in the process and began a friendship that lasted more than 45 years.

The new year—and the new worker—had just begun, but the summer camping program was already calling for attention.

Summertime was filled with camps, most of them conducted by district leadership. The Young People's Secretary, who participated at the invitation of the district, could be assigned to lead conferences, teach a mission study book, bring a missionary message or devotional, direct the GA coronation service, help with crafts and recreation, or "all of the above."

Eula Mae did not have a car so she usually traveled by bus or train. She became increasingly familiar with schedules and

EULA MAE'S FIRST PRESIDENT—Rosalind Smyth (Mrs. Earl B.) served from 1946 to 1949, the first of eight presidents with whom Eula Mae served. Mrs. Smyth was elected at the 1946 Annual Meeting in Mineral Wells, Texas, as was Eula Mae.

fares, as Jimmy Allen, a later Royal Ambassador Secretary was to learn.

And then there was Ridgecrest, a highlight for girls and women. Eula Mae took two busloads of YWAs to the YWA conference at Ridgecrest Assembly her first summer. It was a first in other areas as well: her first time to participate in the Ridgecrest experience and the first time to sponsor two busloads of girls, with the help of other adults. "We had a great time," she recalled later. "But it was also, shall we say, a learning experience. As I look back on it, I think I matured quite a bit during those two weeks. We made the trip just fine, although the buses were not air-conditioned. But then since most were not in those days, we really didn't notice it."

THIS I REMEMBER: I met Eula Mae when she first came to the Baptist Building where I worked in another department as a bookkeeper. The first thought that pops into my head when I hear her name is "she was always my friend." And then I think "cold bread and cold weiners," and I have to smile.

You see, I was one of those YWAs who went with her to Ridgecrest in 1947, and she made an unforgettable impression on me from the beginning. One night after the evening session, we decided we were hungry. We asked her if she wanted something to eat, and she replied, "Yes, surprise me!"

We did—more, perhaps than she had in mind! For what we returned with was cold bread and even colder weiners! Quite a repast, but we all sat on the bed and ate them.

Did Eula Mae get indigestion? No. She got the giggles!

Later, she and I both worked in the Sunday School at First Baptist in Dallas, and our friendship continued through the years. When she passed away, I read in "The Baptist Standard" about the scholarship set up in her name, and I knew right then I wanted to have a part in it as a memorial to her. I did. It was my privilege."
—Jane Scarbrough Johnson

Eula Mae found both of her "bosses," Mrs. Smyth and Mrs. Mathis, to be very supportive. And since Mrs. Mathis had served as Young People's Secretary, she was able to offer special help. State young people's work covered a wide range of ages, each with its own set of opportunities and its own set of questions, as Eula Mae discovered.

The following year Eula Mae found her world changing. In the late spring of 1947, with considerable regret, Mrs. Mathis resigned her position as Executive Secretary-Treasurer to join the staff of First Baptist Church, Dallas. She wrote at the time, "I have been at Headquarters for so long that the work has become a part of me, and I hate to give it up."[4] She indicated that she would work until the end of the convention year. (This she did; two years later, in 1949, she would return as the new state WMU president.)

It was May when Mrs. Mathis resigned. After several months of prayer and soul-searching, the Nominating Committee offered the position to Eula Mae in spite of her youthful years and appearance.

She was as overwhelmed as she had been in 1946 when offered a state position. By this time, she knew enough of the enormity of the task to understand what the work entailed. Her initial reaction was quite similar to what her feelings had been when asked to be Young People's Secretary. On the one hand she felt "The job is too big; I don't think I can do it." On the other, "I think I could learn." The dilemma weighed heavily upon her.

Again she spent time in prayer, and again she sought the counsel of those who were mentors and friends. Ultimately she came to the conclusion that God was leading in this opportunity; that He had been preparing her for this position, and that, as before, she could learn. She still felt personally inadequate, but overriding this was the conviction that "I cannot do it, but God can." She accepted, and was elected at the 1947 convention.

Among the congratulatory messages she received was one from M. Theron Rankin, Executive Secretary of the Foreign Mission Board. "We have had such a pleasant relationship with Mrs. Marie Mathis and Mrs. Olivia Davis before her," he wrote. "We are looking forward to an equally pleasant relationship with you."[5] In that hope he was not disappointed.

Eula Mae's excellent relationship with national leadership was one of the hallmarks of her tenure.

Mrs. Olivia Davis, long a mainstay in Texas WMU and Treasurer since 1925, had retired in 1945, having served with commitment and distinction. Two stalwarts still in the office in those early years were Bernice Caldwell, Eula Mae's secretary, and Nobie McGill, who worked in the mailroom. Along with others, these two were dedicated to missions education, and to Eula Mae. Commenting on it later, Nobie said, "I was always in awe of Miss Henderson, even though she herself seemed to be a little shy in those early years. I heard her when she gave her first talk to the Executive Board because I was in associational work at the time. Also, I remember one state meeting during those early years when she closed the session with prayer. I went up to her and told her, 'If you can pray like that, we don't have anything to worry about!' That's the way I felt."[6]

Nobie described "those days in Texas WMU."

"I remember we worked hard, and under cramped conditions; but I also remember the fun we had at the office birthday parties and on the bus trips with the women to Ridgecrest. On one of these trips, Miss Henderson was running up and down the aisles with a stocking pulled over her face. On another, the air conditioning in the bus broke down, and she was the one who volunteered to sit in the back where it was hottest and take all the bumps."

As Executive Secretary-Treasurer, Eula Mae put her background to work for her. She proved to be a responsible steward of what she had learned. Her days at Hills Business College and Myers Motor Company stood her in good stead in the financial arena. Her time at seminary and at Morgan Avenue Baptist Church gave rise to concepts and ideas she began to share with her staff. The importance of perseverance and attitude came through strongly.

"I recall office meetings when Miss Henderson would talk about attitude," one former staffer recalled. "I really had never thought much about it until she started those little meetings. She talked about how important it was to have a good attitude about everything. She said it wasn't always easy, and she was right. But she also said that if we kept it up, it would make a difference in the work and in us. She was right there too."

Meanwhile, the position of Young People's Secretary was vacant again since Eula Mae had assumed the executive leadership. For a year, until the coming of Ruth Thornton in 1948 to head the young people's work, Eula Mae filled both jobs.

"How did you do it?" she was asked in later years.

"I really don't know," she responded with a laugh. "There just wasn't anyone else, so you just did both jobs, one day at a time. Maybe that's when I started saying 'It doesn't all have to be done today.' I did try to keep in mind and plan for what had to be done on the two levels and, of course, I had wonderful volunteers to help me. Today, I don't think I would even attempt it!"

About this time, since leadership training was one of Mrs. Smyth's emphases, training sessions were offered to women coming to Executive Board meetings. Conferences were held preceding the sessions and free helps distributed to members and guests. Reports given the following year showed the training sessions had yielded results. Sharp increases in all mission offerings were evident and the number of organizations reaching the highest ranking of A-1 was up. Eula Mae presented certificates to the presidents of local WMUs who had achieved the honor and pins to A-1 associational and district presidents.

In 1948, the women rejoiced also in encouraging reports brought by R. A. Springer, Treasurer of the Baptist General Convention of Texas, who told of good work done in rural churches as a result of the Mary Hill Davis Offering. Hal Buckner then told of his projected plan of a home for the aged, a home for unwed mothers, and a ranch school for boys, all to be a part of the Buckner care-giving network.

In that same meeting, the Recording Secretary wrote in

the minutes, "Miss Ruth Thornton, newly-elected Young People's Secretary, was presented to the body." Eula Mae rejoiced! Help had arrived!

In the late 1940s, the work of Royal Ambassadors was still under Woman's Missionary Union. In Texas, the RA Secretary worked with both Eula Mae in Texas WMU and with the Brotherhood Secretary, L. H. Tapscott. Filling that position from 1948 to 1950 was Jimmy Allen, later to become President of the Baptist General Convention of Texas, and President of the Southern Baptist Convention. Additionally, he was to serve as Executive Director of agencies, both on the state and national level.

"I first knew Eula Mae back when she was Young People's Secretary," Dr. Allen recalled. "During those days, I was a Royal Ambassador myself; my mother, a State Approved Worker. I did 'scud work' on mailings from the state WMU office.

"In the early days of my RA tenure, I worked full time in the summer with a team of four to organize and direct boys' camps, one after another, for 13 weeks in different sections of the state. During the academic year, I was in classes at the seminary four days a week, and at work with the RA program during the three-day weekends. I was twenty years old at the time."

Chapter 3   29

THIS I REMEMBER: In my two years as Royal Ambassador Secretary in Texas (1948-1950), camps were a highlight. The WMUs of the area would invite us and I would take in my camp team at no expense to the local group. I little realized at the time that the pastors and laymen who showed up to work with us were not the people who had invited me, and who had agreed to my methods of working. This made for tension every Monday as camp began. I was in charge, but I was just a kid barely out of his teens, invited by folks who weren't even there. Undaunted, I moved in and held my ground on agreements.

Eula Mae had to deal with whatever backlash I created. To her credit, I never heard a word of complaint from her. I was doing what she asked me to do, and she took care of it. I only heard later the problems I had created, and I learned them from other sources.

She taught me a lesson on leadership by her example. She was capable of "quoting the book" when called for, but she supported her people in their tasks.
—Jimmy Allen

"I had received an invitation to lead conferences in El Paso and that conjured up in my mind pictures of another airline trip. I was hopping airplanes with increasing regularity and Eula Mae was casting a concerned eye on my expense account. I breezed into her office with airline schedules and prices in hand for the El Paso trip. She glanced at the material, then looked up at me and asked calmly, 'Have you considered the train?'

"I was stunned! The train! Hours of being bored while rocking mile after mile across the desert raced through my mind. I sputtered, 'No, I hadn't thought of that.' Eula Mae smiled, and laid out a train schedule for me. It showed that I could ride eleven hours overnight and save twelve dollars. Oh well, I reasoned, I needed the time with my books and typewriter anyway."

Dr. Allen concludes by saying, "She was gracious yet firm, an exacting person, totally focused on missions. She was also frugal with mission money!"[7]

Eula Mae, ever a reader, was systematically broadening her reading menu. Included were missions materials, denominational publications, and devotional books. Probably her favorite in the latter category was Oswald Chambers' *My Utmost for His Highest*, which she read several times, underlined, and wrote comments in the margins. Other favorite authors included Sidlow Baxter, Andrew Murray, Georgia Harkness, and Corrie ten Boom.

Her speaking skills, already well above average, were being honed as well. Her report to the Executive Board in September 1949 began, "Georgia Harkness has made this statement: 'We live in a world in which multitudes of people regard the gospel neither as good news nor bad news. To them, it is no news. They do not reject it. They simply ignore it.'" She went on to state how this problem was being addressed in Texas.

And then followed several sentences with the picturesque language, the verbal pictures, that were to become one of her trademarks as a speaker. "Though we have some who seemingly live on prejudice peak, on ignorance island, in selfish state, or contented country, there are many who live in an environment saturated with missions thought and missions work." She went on to tell of 48 new missionary societies that had been reported in the last four months. She visualized these women studying about rural and Hispanic churches in Texas, and then giving to the Mary Hill Davis Offering to support these churches. She pictured them learning about *Japan's New Day*, and then giving to the Lottie Moon Christmas Offering. She saw them as new tithers, as participating in planned community missions, and as taking part in all phases of the work.[8]

In conclusion, she gave the women a glimpse of other aspects of her work as Executive Secretary-Treasurer: "In March, I attended a Home Mission Board conference in Albuquerque and visited some of the home mission fields in New Mexico, Arizona, and California. In May, I attended the WMU Convention and the Southern Baptist Convention in Oklahoma City. In August, I went to Ridgecrest for WMU Week and led a daily conference for Young People's Secretaries. Back in Texas I met with the Methods and Finance Committee twice, the Report and Record Book Committee, and with Dr. J. Howard Williams and committee twice in planning the upcoming stewardship rallies."[9]

Two years into the work as Executive Secretary-Treasurer, Eula Mae was creating her own plan of work.

In 1949, Mrs. Smyth resigned the presidency of Texas WMU because of health problems, and Marie Mathis was elected. Eula Mae and "Mrs. M," as EMH called her, were now in a different relationship and one that was to further the teamwork approach.

Mrs. Mathis was not only an attractive woman, but she was also charming and creative. Additionally, she was a motivator and a diplomat. Her knowledge of missions and her leadership skills had been finely honed by the time she came to the state presidency.

THIS I REMEMBER: Mrs. Mathis was a woman of many talents, many capabilities. Certainly she impressed a number of people, and I was among them.

Although she was quite approachable, and asked me to call her "Marie," I just couldn't bring myself to do it. Maybe it's because she was "way up there" when I was new in the work, I don't know. Anyway, I couldn't say "Marie." It wouldn't come out.

So she was always "Mrs. M" to me. I guess after a while, she got used to it, because she never mentioned it again.
—Eula Mae Henderson

Eula Mae learned a great deal from her. "She was the sort of person who believed that things could be done and set about doing them," Eula Mae said, recalling one of their times together when a state convention was in the offing. The two women had gone to the city auditorium where the meetings were to be held and Mrs. Mathis was discussing the staging with the stage manager.

After she described what she had in mind, his response was, "Well, now, that can't be done."

She replied with something like, "I can see how there might be a problem, but this is so important to our program. Can you help us? Tell me how you think we can work this out."

They talked some more, and after a while the answer was forthcoming, something they both agreed on. Mrs. Mathis knew how to listen, how to understand someone else's position, and how to work things out together.

Eula Mae was a learner, as she had hoped to be. Along the

pathway, she looked, listened, and learned. And then she passed it on to others.

To do so was a responsibility, a privilege, a part of what she sometimes called "the larger stewardship."

The 1950 Annual Meeting led by the Mathis-Henderson duo proved to be the first of many outstanding events. Held in Will Rogers Auditorium in Fort Worth, preceding the Baptist General Convention of Texas yearly meeting, the sessions were characterized by meaningful worship periods, challenging speakers, inspirational music, dramatized reports, and spectacular staging.

Speakers included Mrs. J. M. Dawson, formerly of Texas but now of Washington, D.C.; Mrs. C. D. Creasman of WMU, SBC; Samuel Maddox of the Foreign Mission Board; R. G. Lee of Tennessee; and Loyd Corder of the Home Mission Board. Dr. Corder was assisted by "Joe Baptist," a wooden dummy who frequently accompanied him, and who made remarks that no real person could say. This decidedly caught the attention of the audience.

Missionaries featured included Letha Saunders, Brazil; Mrs. Maurice Brantley, Nigeria; Finlay Graham, Lebanon; and Eugene Hill, China.

Worship periods were led by Mrs. Woodson Armes, Mrs. Robert Neff, Mrs. B. A. Copass, and Miss Betty Chong. Sunbeams, GAs, and RAs also participated, working under the direction of Ruth Thornton and Jimmy Allen.

Floy Barnard of Southwestern Baptist Theological Seminary presented "The Judsons," which she dedicated to Miss Thornton and the young people of Texas.

Music was led by BO Baker of Fort Worth, with Earl Miller of Dallas at the organ; Mrs. David Gardner of Dallas and Mrs. Jack Terrell of Houston were at the pianos.

Registration at the meeting showed that 3,690 were present, including messengers, visitors, and missionaries.[10]

It was an unforgettable "first time around" for the new Texas WMU team.

4

Horizons Unlimited . . . at Home and Abroad

"I spent 41 never-to-be-forgotten days touring the mission fields of South America with Alma Hunt. I came home with a greater love for missionaries, a greater knowledge of the work of the Lottie Moon Christmas Offering, and a greater desire to share with our people our missions opportunities."

Standing to address the Executive Board of Woman's Missionary Union of Texas in September 1951, the slender young woman with the dark curly hair was excited.

She showed it. Her brown eyes showed it. They sparkled. So did she.

Since late 1947 she had been Executive Secretary-Treasurer, and now she had made her first mission trip overseas. Glowingly she spoke of her trip, as she was to do often in the months ahead.

"I spent 41 never-to-be-forgotten days touring the mission fields of South America with Alma Hunt." Gratefully, she thanked Texas WMU for providing such a trip, for making this investment in her future and in theirs. Happily she recounted highlights of the days.

Certainly her traveling companion, Alma Hunt, Executive Secretary for Woman's Missionary Union, auxiliary to the Southern Baptist Convention, shared her enthusiasm as well as providing sideline details of Eula Mae in action.

35

"One of the things I remember the most about the trip was Eula Mae's consistent interest in not only the mission work we saw, but the missionaries themselves," Alma recalled. "That interest was genuine. People sensed it and responded to her. I saw it then, and I saw it in later years as she worked on both the state and national levels.

"That particular trip was my first overseas mission trip also, and probably set a pattern for what was to follow. For both Eula Mae and me, there were many highlights. For example, I recall our visit to Rosario, Argentina, a special time for us both. Anne Sowell Margrett had met us, and taken us to a reception that afternoon. There we had the privilege of shaking hands with history because Mrs. Ella Good Hosford was there. Many years earlier, the Hosfords—Ella and Robert—had journeyed from Rosario to Buenos Aires to meet Sidney Sowell (who later became Anne's father) when he disembarked to begin Southern Baptist work in Argentina. Both Eula Mae and I were captivated by the lady and by her story. Incidentally, she was a grandmother of Laurella Owens, who later edited *Royal Service*.

"Like others before us, we were impressed with the beauty of Argentina. I recall Buenos Aires and the abundant use of marble in both public buildings and private residences. At the time we were there, Evita Peron was very much in the national consciousness; you could see her name scrawled in big black letters on some of that beautiful white marble.

"Trips like ours usually have their humorous sidelights and ours was no exception. On one occasion, Eula Mae's lack of Spanish kept her from getting a much-needed drink of water; instead the bellboy brought her about an inch of water in a glass to brush her teeth. I could add also that Eula Mae is the only person I know who could turn a beautiful blue suit into dusty red. I do mean dusty! She walked through the Charcarita section of Asunción, Paraguay, with missionary nurse Miriam Willis; and the journey through those unpaved streets, with dust swirling everywhere, decidedly changed the color of that lovely suit!"[1]

The work of Texas WMU picked up with renewed vigor the day she returned. Her mission trip had sharpened her awareness of opportunities on both sides of the ocean. In the 1951 report in which she spoke so glowingly of her mission trip, she also summarized some of the "at home" highlights.

"In the 189 days since last we met, I have had the opportunity to be in 14 of our 17 districts. During April, I assisted with 12 WMU district conferences; more than 7,300 women attended these meetings." Appreciation was expressed to Mrs. C. D. Creasman and Miss Margaret Bruce, both WMU, SBC for the contribution they made to the meetings.

"Besides the usual correspondence, I have prepared *Baptist Standard* articles each week, and (worked on) the Texas WMU Yearbook, the Report and Record Book, two issues of *The Helper*, the Week of Prayer for State Missions, the Ministerial Relief Program, and a suggested associational WMU report. I have met with the Christian Life Commission and assisted in planning the WMU program for the state-wide evangelistic meeting held on September 4. I have planned for the district conventions in November, securing Mrs. William McMurry and Miss Edith Stokely from WMU, SBC for these meetings, as well as Miss Jaxie Short of Hong Kong. Either Mrs. R.L. Mathis, Miss Ruth Thornton, or myself will (be the additional member of each team)."

Then followed the statistical report of the six-month period, noting that 13,225 letters had been received, and 6,241 literature orders filled, not including week of prayer materials. These, together with Ministerial Relief materials and packets to local presidents, numbered another 11,470.[2]

THIS I REMEMBER: *After the mission trip to South America, I was in Texas for a state convention. I came to the auditorium and asked for Eula Mae. I was told she was standing between the two curtains; the meeting was about to start.*

I went to greet her and then stopped short. We were wearing identical dresses, complete with a pin on the left shoulder!

Mrs. Mathis, presiding at the convention, noticed this at once. She thought the situation hilarious, and asked me to stand beside Eula Mae when she came to give her report. I did so.

When the audience saw us standing there looking like the Bobbsey twins, they roared. And so did we!
—Alma Hunt

Such was the work of the Executive Secretary-Treasurer in the early 1950s.

But Eula Mae enjoyed the work and cherished her relationship with co-workers, both in WMU circles and other areas of denominational effort. "It was structured less formally in those earlier years than what it was later," she said, recalling the 1950s. "As the work grew, so did the structure. It had to. When I came, J. Howard Williams was Executive Secretary; he certainly had the affection and respect of Texas Baptists, as have those who followed after him. At that time in Texas Baptist work, we had districts and district missionaries, 17 of them, and those 17 men appreciated Dr. Williams and his leadership. He was especially strong in the areas of stewardship and tithing, and was a warm, easy-to-know individual."[3]

Since there were fewer departments of work, Dr. Williams would call the leadership "to meet in my office tomorrow afternoon," Eula Mae remembered. There was no need to arrange staff meetings weeks or months in advance. "Come," Dr. Williams would say, "and we'll talk."

The group would assemble and Dr. Williams would say, "Tell us something about your work. Tell us what you're doing." Thus encouraged, T. C. Gardner would discuss Training Union, Andrew Allen, the Sunday School, L. H. Tapscott, the Brotherhood, Eula Mae, the WMU, and thus the meeting would go.

"We'd just go around the table," Eula Mae said. "It wasn't a structured meeting; it was very informal."[4]

Even in those early days, Eula Mae stressed that "Texas WMU was organized as an auxiliary to the Baptist General Convention of Texas. Remember, 'auxiliary' means 'helper.' I think we have always been that, working closely with the BGCT Executive Secretary (later Director) and leaders of other areas of work in the Baptist Building. The executive directors through the years have always included me in staff meetings, in asking us to give a report to the convention, and so forth. Ours has been an excellent working relationship."[5]

The informality of the early days gave way to more structured procedures as Texas Baptists mushroomed in the 1950s, and hosts of new churches came into being. When Dr. Williams resigned as Executive Secretary to become President of Southwestern Baptist Theological Seminary, he was succeeded by Forrest Feezor. He was "A big man in body and spirit," said Eula Mae. "If you were a man and ever shook hands with him, you never forgot it! He often started with his right arm high in the air behind him, then brought it down and forward with considerable force to meet your outstretched hand. I used to enjoy watching him do it. Unforgettable—especially if you were on the receiving end!"

Much about those days was memorable. Eula Mae often quoted the psalmist who said, "My lines have fallen in pleasant places," for indeed she felt they had. Her work was both a joy and a challenge, and her home life equally pleasant. Shortly after moving to Dallas, she had rented a room in the home of Dr. and Mrs. H. E. Fowler at 6200 Belmont Street, not far from White Rock Lake. Dr. Fowler served on the staff of First Baptist Church in Dallas as an associate pastor and the entire family was active in the church.

Very quickly Eula Mae was accepted as a member of the family, taking breakfast with the Fowlers, then staying in town for lunch and dinner. On Sunday, the family went together to First Baptist Church where Eula Mae had also placed her membership. She began working in one of the Junior Sunday School departments, a position she was to hold for some 30 years.

When Eula Mae first rented a room from the Fowlers, a son and daughter were also at home—Sterling and AvaNell. Eula Mae was like a big sister to AvaNell; and since, for family reasons lost in genealogical mists, the parents called AvaNell "Little Judy," they began to call Eula Mae "Big Judy." The nickname stayed within the Fowler family until 1953.

Chapter 4

THIS I REMEMBER: *Eula Mae's lighter side popped up unexpectedly at times—so unexpectedly that I found myself hard-pushed to keep up with her. Sometimes I just didn't!*

One day about the mid-fifties, she and I were just finishing a late lunch in downtown Dallas and stepped out on one of the main streets to see a large elephant placidly swaying from side to side on the sidewalk directly across the street from us.

We both stopped short. Then, never taking her eyes off the huge beast, Eula Mae said slowly in an unbelieving voice, "I do hope you see an elephant!"

Mesmerized, I replied in the same incredulous tone, "Yes, I do; and I'm worried about both of us!"

I just didn't think fast enough. I do wish I had turned to her and said with a straight face, "No, I don't. Is there one? Where?"

She would have loved it.

So much for quick thinking!

Upon investigation, it turned out that a theater was showing a jungle film, and this was one of their advertising ploys.

—Millie Bishop

Having no car, Eula Mae became quite familiar with the Dallas transit system, riding the Live Oak bus to and from work, properly attired in the requisite hat and gloves. Of course, these necessary items came off when she started to work, but the hat went back on when lunchtime came. Food was important to her and she had learned of several good eating places in the downtown area. One of her favorites was a health food store where she ordered yogurt, a spinach salad, and garbonzos. Another favorite from the other end of the nutritional scale was Mexican food. She also enjoyed desserts and, with her slender figure, could well afford to eat them. Usually she worked after closing time to "give herself a good start in the morning," then enjoyed a downtown meal before she caught the bus home.

Socializing usually involved co-workers or friends. On occasion she dated single pastors whose paths had crossed hers; usually this was a dinner event. As often as her schedule permitted, she caught the train to Oklahoma City to visit her parents and her sister, Erma. Vacations were frequently taken in connection with the Southern Baptist Convention, either a few days before or a few days after the sessions.

Often she made the same comment about these days as she had about her time in Corpus Christi: "Those were good days; I enjoyed them." And then she would add with a bit of a smile, "But these are good days too! And I enjoy them also!"

The year 1951 was memorable for many reasons other than EMH's first mission trip. It was also the year when Texas Baptists, for the first time, gave more than a million dollars to the Lottie Moon Christmas Offering. Of course, gifts to the offering extended over into 1952, as was true in subsequent years. On April 23, 1952, a check was written for one million dollars, made out to the Executive Committee of the Southern Baptist Convention. At the time, it was the largest single check written by any Baptist group.[6]

There was rejoicing in the state office and throughout Texas. The check represented all Texas Baptists, not just the WMU. For several years, Mrs. Mathis and Eula Mae had been promoting the idea of churchwide offerings, with the WMU in local churches having the responsibility for leading out in observing the weeks of prayer and in the ingathering of the attendant offerings.

Texas WMU publications were also expanding. By the early 1950s, EMH and her co-workers had come up with the idea for *The Helperette*, an insert for *The Helper*, which had been started in 1945. The new insert, with material prepared by Ruth Thornton and Jimmy Allen, promoted the young people's organizations.

This area of work, in fact, was increasingly in the spotlight. Sunbeams, Girls' Auxiliary and Young Woman's Auxiliary provided a popular highlight for associational, district, and state programs. Sometimes the children involved were from Texas Baptist children's homes. By the following year, there were four such institutions caring for nearly 1,000 children, marking "a long trail" from that day in 1880 when R. C. Buckner began an orphanage in a rented cottage in Dallas. Included were Buckner Orphans Home, Dallas; Texas Baptist Children's Home, Round Rock; Mexican Baptist Children's Home, San Antonio; and a new one, South Texas Baptist Children's Home, Beeville.[7]

Promotion of the work included something new in the early 1950s. Radio Station KYBS-FM, Dallas, heard within a radius of 150 miles, carried a Texas state WMU radio program each Monday morning from 10:30 to 10:45. The record shows that Eula Mae and Ruth Thornton had the honor of doing many of the programs.[8]

Meanwhile, looking ahead, Texas WMU leadership noted that the organization would celebrate its 75th birthday in 1955. Hence, in 1952, a special committee was appointed to prepare for the event. Heading the group was Mrs. A. A. Cummins, working with Mrs. H. C. Wigger, Mrs. T. A. Patterson, Mrs. Henry Heck, Mrs. E. Hob Smith, and Mrs. N. B. Moon. Plans began for "the biggest and best," climaxing with a "real live pageant" in the Houston coliseum in the autumn of 1955.

44   Lengthening Legacy: Eula Mae Henderson

AND THE WMU NEWS OF THE DAY IS . . .—Eula Mae broadcasts the weekly State WMU radio program heard on Station KYBS-FM on Mondays in the early 1950s. The Dallas station was heard within a radius of 150 miles.

Ruth Thornton had married Lawson Pritchett in 1952, and in 1953 resigned as Young People's Secretary to join her chaplain husband in Tokyo. Her successor was Amelia (Millie) Morton (later Mrs. J. Ivyloy Bishop) who graduated from Southwestern Baptist Theological Seminary in May 1953. Coming from a journalism and drama background, Millie became the writing arm of the Mathis-Henderson-Morton team, and also assisted Mrs. Mathis with staging.

Millie moved to Dallas and, having initially no place to live, was invited by the Fowlers to rent an extra room in their home with the same arrangement they had with Eula Mae. She did so, thinking of it as temporary. In reality, she and Eula Mae both rented rooms there for several months until they took an upper duplex together in the same neighborhood. Millie began to call Eula Mae "Judy" as did the Fowlers; some WMU staffers also picked up the nickname.

Neither Eula Mae nor Millie had a car; they rode the bus. They both liked yogurt and Mexican food, but realized that a nutritious diet required something in between, so they worked at it. They took turns cooking, occasionally hosting friends for dinner. Neither had much furniture, and so they decided that each would buy certain items they needed. At first, Eula Mae did not think that a television set was necessary, but then changed her mind rather abruptly on a field trip. She heard a group of the women discussing a popular program and understood the name to be "I Love Loosely." This puzzled her until she listened further, and discovered that the correct name was "I Love Lucy," and she had never heard of it. "I realized I was certainly out of touch," she said later. "That day, I decided that we needed a TV!"

In September 1953, the Methods and Finance Committee recommended "That we send a group of state officers, state chairmen, and approved workers to Louisiana in January

1954, in the interest of home missions and the Annie Armstrong Offering."⁹

The adult and young people's home missions books for 1954 featured Louisiana, with emphasis on the Evangeline Country. Consequently, the group concentrated on that part of the state, traveling in two leased Chevrolets. Drivers were Robert Chapman, RA Secretary, who had been elected in 1953, and Millie Morton. The group visited churches and mission points, interviewed missionaries, ate Cajun cooking, and took voluminous color slides to share with the folks back home.

Each day, Eula Mae had a fruit-basket-turnover list to indicate which participant rode in which car. In addition to Mrs. Mathis, Eula Mae, and the drivers, others making the trip included Mrs. H. C. Hunt, Mrs. L. N. Yaeger, Mrs. Herbert Clark, Mrs. Tom Drewett, Mrs. Robert Fling, Mrs. Lee Stephens, Mrs. R. L Brown, and Mrs. L. W. Terrell. (The latter was Opel Terrell, who claimed as she described her early years in WMU, "I had enough ignorance to ignorance the whole state!")

The money spent to finance the trip proved to be a good investment. As group members traveled throughout Texas in subsequent weeks, interest in home missions was quickened, and giving to the Annie Armstrong Offering increased.

Recalling the trip in later years, Eula Mae would comment on the richness of the experience, and then, typically, add interesting sidelights. "I remember visiting with one home missionary when her niece was also present. The little girl simply walked in the room, held out her hand and, without mentioning her own name, identified herself by saying, 'I am my aunt's niece!' That was a real compliment; it said it all!

"I also remember the homemade pralines that missionary Lawrence Thibodeaux enjoyed making—and we enjoyed eating! I recall Helen Fling's comment the first time she ate pompano en papillote. She took one bite, chewed slowly, swallowed, and then said with a dreamy look in her eyes, 'I just want to die with this taste in my mouth!'

"And I guess none of us will ever forget the time that the road to our destination was unpaved and swamp-like. Our cautious drivers kept going slower and slower. 'Just don't stop,' said the missionary guide in the lead car. 'If you do, you'll sink!' Needless to say, the cars didn't stop!"[10]

An ongoing emphasis of Eula Mae's administration manifested early was her attention to the young people's programs, illustrated by her total support of all phases of the work. Perhaps this was because she understood the importance of "investing our todays for their tomorrows." Perhaps it was because she herself had so recently led young people's work and understood the needs of the program and how to be helpful; perhaps it was both. At any rate, her support was unwavering. She stayed in the background during the event unless given a program responsibility. However, her presence was felt and she became a part of the linkage to the years ahead.

One example was the YWA House Party held February 1954, at Mary Hardin-Baylor College (now University). Interest in these events was high; this year was no exception. The program was centered around "Love Is the Theme" and included such luminaries as Sybil Leonard Armes, always a favorite, and soloist June Cooper, later a missionary to Japan. The several hundred girls who attended were entranced—one in particular.

Her name was Joy. She was an 18-year-old college freshman who had been enlisted in Young Woman's Auxiliary by a new friend. Joy did not have a church background, so she knew very little about YWA except that it meant much to the friend who had invited her. Also, she did not have the money to attend; she worked on campus for a whopping forty cents an hour, which took care of room and board, but no extras. However, she decided to use her food money to attend. When she arrived, she found out she had been awarded a scholarship for the event, which strengthened the idea that she was "in the right place at the right time."

She was. The House Party opened a whole world of missions education—the missionaries, the drama, the music, the teaching, the fellowship—all planned by the state leadership. That YWA involvement led Joy to say "yes" when asked later to be a leader in Girls' Auxiliary in her local church.

That was the beginning. Her name was Joy Phillips, and the same Joy who later became state GA Director, then the wife of Charlie Fenner and a missionary to Japan; and in 1980, the Executive Director-Treasurer to follow Eula Mae.

It all tied together. Linkage.

Other special events came into focus as Texas WMU looked forward to 1955, the year of the organization's Diamond Jubilee.

"All of us, starting with Mrs. Mathis, wanted to try things we had never done before," Eula Mae recalled. "One was the idea of having four regional conventions in the spring of 1954 to help us get ready for our big year. Of course we had held regional meetings before, but what we had in mind now was to be a convention-format meeting—sometimes we called them 'conventionettes,' and they were all focused on getting us ready for our 75th anniversary. We also included a presentation of the Standard of Excellence, our plan of work at that time."[11]

The four events were held in March and April 1954, in Big Spring, Harlingen, Tyler, and Waco. The program was the same in each meeting, featuring an all-inclusive, two-hour session in the morning, followed by a fellowship luncheon. Program personalities in one or more of the meetings included not only state officers and chairmen, but also Edith Stokely of what was then called "Southern Union" (WMU, SBC), Helen Falls of New Orleans Baptist Theological Seminary, Sybil Leonard Armes of Fort Worth, and Kenneth Aufill, a Margaret Fund student at Hardin-Simmons University.

"The program was identical, but the stage and luncheon decorations were quite different," Eula Mae recalled. "In Big Spring, the women used tumbleweeds sprayed silver across the front of the stage, whereas in Harlingen, they used bougainvillea and Mexican artifacts; in Tyler, it was a profusion of flowers, and in Waco, beautiful hydrangeas."

"Our staging was unique, especially in view of the fact that it had to be taken down after each meeting, and shipped to the next place. We had a large replica of the Texas Year Book in center stage for a portion of the program, and our state chairmen entered through it to give their reports. It worked just fine, but I remember that one of our people was confused as to how that large piece of staging could be moved from city to city for our three meetings to follow. She made the mistake of asking Millie Morton about it. Millie, with a perfectly straight face replied, 'That huge year book comes apart in seven-inch pieces and can easily be shipped." Whereupon the questioner walked up to the year book, surveyed it from top to bottom, and gingerly felt up and down its smooth surface to find the seven-inch pieces. Obviously they weren't there. She turned back to Millie in confusion. By this time, the Young People's Secretary was struggling to keep her composure and had to confess that she had somewhat misled her fellow worker."[12]

The questioner was Helen Fling. Later, she became quite familiar with all types of staging in Oklahoma and New York, as well as WMU, SBC, where she served as national President from 1963 to 1969.

THIS I REMEMBER: Indeed I remember much about Eula Mae, from the early fifties, on down.

She was a splendid role model for all of us in so many different areas. An effective and fair administrator who had a loving interest in each co-worker, she built an incredible rapport among officers, staff members, office personnel, and volunteers. Hers was the talent of bestowing dignity and position upon every woman who attempted to obey the Great Commission.

As a state chairman in the early fifties, I felt both the joy and responsibility of my work as if I had been on the payroll. Eula Mae was unsurpassed in planning programs and conferences, and this included attention to details. She was specific in instructions, yet she was the soul of tact. One of her favorite phrases at House Party time was, "You will help us if you will dismiss your conference on time, and reconvene promptly for the general session."

You may be sure I would not have kept my conference overtime for one minute!
—Helen Fling

The conventionettes, while they served their purpose in promoting the upcoming Diamond Jubilee Celebration, were just one of several avenues leading up to the big year. Another was a so-called one-time event conceived by Mrs. Mathis and Eula Mae and tabbed "The House Party."

"It was really planned as a one-time occasion," Eula Mae explained. "We were trying to pull out all the stops to get ready for 1955. Hence the idea of a one-time, state-wide event seemed good to us. In our initial thinking, it would be held in a camp setting."

At this juncture, one of those mix-ups transpired that has grown larger and funnier through the years. "Mrs. Mathis came to the office one day—it must have been late winter or early spring—and said that she thought a camp would be much too hot in mid-summer for a state-wide meeting," Eula Mae recalled. "She was thinking of moving the event to Baylor University, if it could be worked out and asked our opinion.

"I had no objection, but Millie did. She thought about it for a minute, then said 'The House Party is a great idea, but I don't believe you can change the site of such a big event at this late date and still get good results. You might want to leave it where it is.'

"What is so funny about this is that, through the years, Millie has been quoted as saying 'The House Party won't work.' She laughs about it now, since it became our largest state meeting, and remarks, 'Either way, quoted or misquoted, I was wrong. It did work, and it did work to move it! Just look at the results!'"[13]

When the summer of 1954 rolled around, the first Texas WMU House Party was indeed held at Baylor University, with some 1,500 women in attendance. This was decidedly more than had been expected, and some WMUers who attended that first event have a mental picture of Eula Mae standing up on a table in the middle of the registration area. She was issuing on-the-spot instructions to bring order to the milling throngs when registration workers were overwhelmed.

The format of the meeting at that time was to open on Tuesday evening, and close at Friday noon. In the first few years, state-wide fellowships were held for two of the three nights, following the evening session. Texas was still divided into 17 districts; nine of these would put on a three-minute skit the first night and the remainder, the following night. Each district was responsible for its own presentation. Several stars were born during these hours, including Marge Caldwell, then of Houston, and Wanda Allen, wife of Jimmy Allen.

"The women seemed to truly enjoy these evenings—in fact, all the House Party!" was Eula Mae's comment later.

The year was 1954, and the Diamond Jubilee was on its way. Texas WMU adopted Annie Armstrong's famous cry: "Forward!"

5

Diamond Jubilee . . . and Jubilant Days

"Many women are interested in antiques, and it seems that this year I have admired many dated shoes, bags, pieces of costume jewelry, hats, bonnets, dresses . . . starting in the district meetings in November and continuing through the January associational meetings with the Jubilee programs."

The date was March 1955. The Diamond Jubilee—the 75th anniversary of Texas WMU—was in full swing, and Eula Mae, her dark hair slightly tinged with gray at the temples, was happily sharing with members of the Executive Board. "Certainly we want to express again our appreciation to the members of the 75th Anniversary Committee, and to the committees who planned for the special district and associational programs. No two of these have been alike, but each has carried out the general theme of the Diamond Jubilee."[1]

Seventy-five years. Could it be? Yes!

And enthusiasm bubbled up—local, associational, district, state. It was contagious.

The 75th Anniversary Committee, appointed in 1952, had done its work well. In addition to the 1954 House Party held to prepare for the Jubilee year, specific 75th anniversary plans and goals had been set up for associational, district, and state levels. The watchword selected was meaningful indeed: "Hitherto hath the Lord helped us." The hymn selected was

"Lead On, O King Eternal," and the slogan, "Saved to Serve." Goals had been set for an increase in membership in circles, and special emphases were included in community missions, mission study, stewardship, and young people's work. Additionally, a history of Texas WMU featuring, not only its 75 years, but those activities and influences that had led to organization, had been beautifully written by Roberta Turner Patterson (Mrs. T. A.) and titled *Candle by Night*.

The celebration year had begun in January during WMU Focus Week in a colorful and distinctive fashion with a Diamond Jubilee feature in the churches.

"It was quite a treat," Eula Mae recalled later, "to see all those women in their 1880 costumes, and of course it aroused a lot of interest in the churches. Then, later on, the same costumes appeared in associational and district meetings. The programs included such a variety of features and skits, I found myself wishing I could be in all the meetings!"

Something of a bonus gift took place in the spring in the form of a World Missions Conference, the first sponsored by the Baptist General Convention of Texas and Texas WMU. Some 75 missionaries attended. The second state WMU House Party came in August of that year, held at Baylor University as the first had been, and featured the theme "The Roads We Travel."

Climaxing the anniversary year was the Annual Meeting in Houston. On Tuesday a luncheon was held with more than a thousand women present in the Emerald Room of the Shamrock-Hilton Hotel. Many of those attending were attired in costumes of 1880 vintage—some authentic, some copies—but all colorful, according to the minutes of that day. Appropriately enough, several longtime WMUers took part in the program, including Mrs. T. C. Jester, who had served as Young People's Secretary and College Correspondent from 1926 to 1935; Mrs. Hans Busch, life member of the Texas WMU Executive Board; Mrs. Olivia Davis, former WMU Executive-Treasurer, and Mrs. T. E., Cannedy, longtime life member of the Executive Board.

Since Mrs. Mathis was completing her six years in the presidency, Irene (Mrs. James) Landes of Wichita Falls presented her with several gifts on behalf of Texas WMU. "Mrs. M," whose creative mind had sparked many of the special features of the anniversary year, challenged the women in her closing message, "Lord, Teach Us . . . To Pray, To Study, To Give, To Go."

Always wanting to express appreciation to those who so richly deserved it, Eula Mae recognized those WMUs on the local, associational, and district levels who were eligible for Diamond Awards. She also thanked again Mrs. A. A. Cummins who had chaired the Anniversary Committee, along with the three state chairmen who had included anniversary goals in their areas of work: Mrs. Lon V. Smith, Community Missions; Mrs. Robert Fling, Mission Study, and Mrs. Lee Stephens, Stewardship.

Many of the women also wore their costumes to the Tuesday night session, a combined meeting of Texas WMU and the BGCT in the Houston Coliseum. Featured that night was a pageant depicting the 75-year history of missions in Texas written by Ramsey Yelvington.

"That was a 'first ever' in many ways," Eula Mae said. "Mr. Yelvington did a beautiful job. Both Mrs. Mathis and I marveled at his grasp of what we wanted to depict and the authenticity with which he portrayed it—not to mention the cast of hundreds, all those costumes, the sets and, of course, the horse-drawn covered wagons!"

Like many such mammoth productions, the happenings backstage during the hours preceding the performance made a story all their own.

"Members of numerous Baptist churches were involved in the production," said Louise Yelvington (Denham), who was married to Ramsey and served as one of the narrators for the pageant. (Several years after Ramsey's death, she married William Denham.) "Each of the church groups had rehearsed separately, but not together. In the wings, hundreds of people had gathered, discussing their parts, laughing and talking. Each church group was identified by a sign held aloft, and around the area were a number of larger signs which read 'We are doing the impossible! Please help us by being quiet!'

"But not until a strong voice came through the megaphone

repeating these very words did the crowd settle down. Then, as a result of excellent organizing, it all began to come together."

THIS I REMEMBER: One of the most challenging experiences of my life came in 1955 when I participated in the pageant depicting the history of missions in Texas. It was written by my husband, Ramsey Yelvington, and staged in the Houston Coliseum. We needed four narrators. Ramsey was one, then there was a local speech teacher, a radio announcer, and a lady selected partly for her Southern accent. It turned out she was too Southern; hence, just hours before the performance, she had to be replaced.

Ramsey explained this to me, then gave me a direct look. I knew what was coming. "You'll have to do it," he said.

As a Christian, a Baptist, and a dutiful wife, I did not flinch, but I had reservations about both my ability and the time limit.

"We'll go down to the horse barn and run through it," Ramsey said. We did so, sitting on a huge bale of hay left over from the rodeo. "Watch your diction," Ramsey instructed me. "When you're tired, you say 'Tez-izz' instead of 'Texas.'"

We rehearsed for six or seven hours, ate a hurried meal, then climbed into the broadcast booth.

The time had come. Ramsey put his hand on my back as I read. If I needed to pick up the pace, he beat a quick, gentle staccato; if I was too fast, it was soft measured thumps; to get me to read louder, he pressed down hard; to read more softly, he touched me gently, but firmly.

Before 7,000 people, we did it!

—Louise Yelvington (Denham)

It wasn't an easy pageant to produce. In the center of the arena were three large circles, arranged like a circus, but with the activity of one overlapping the activity of another. "In one scene that I remember," said Mrs. Denham, "a horse-drawn covered wagon which was to carry pioneers was winding its way around one of the circles as though it were on a country road. But it wasn't. It was rolling across a flat floor with a half inch of sand. And there were problems!

"I was in an office with Marie Mathis as she poured over production notes. The clock was ticking away toward curtain time when a young man came in and said, 'Mrs. Mathis, the wagon turns over every time we make that turn! And there are going to be people in it!'"

She looked up and asked, "What would it take to hold the wagon steady?" Her voice was calm, unperturbed, oddly at variance with the tension in the coliseum.

"Another whole load of sand," he answered.

"Order it!" she responded immediately. "At this late date, we do what it takes, and we certainly can't have anyone hurt!"

The sand was ordered. It worked; and one by one, the last-minute problems were worked out.²

The pageant was a magnificent climax to the Diamond Jubilee Annual Meeting.

Meanwhile, the anniversary year was going on, and so was the usual work, and at times, the unusual.

The latter had come several months before in the form of a request from J. M. Price, dean of the Religious Education School of Southwestern Baptist Theological Seminary. Writing to Eula Mae and Amelia Morton, Dr. Price had asked the two of them to teach a Thursday night course in WMU at the seminary during the spring semester. It was suggested that the two might alternate the Thursdays.

"We wanted to do it for Woman's Missionary Union and

for the seminary," Eula Mae said. "But we really didn't see how we could. Thursday has a way of coming around every week, and in addition to our usual programs and activities, this was the anniversary year!"

However, the two prospective professors talked with Mrs. Mathis about the opportunity, and she encouraged them to take it, if at all possible. They then wrote to Dr. Price, asking for more information on how all of it might work. To their surprise, he wrote back, thanking them for accepting.

"Before we knew it, Thursdays did begin to roll around," Eula Mae said later. "We decided to team teach, so we both went each Thursday. It was a large class. About 80 were enrolled, both men and women. We also had one Black pastor, Marvin Griffin, who later became Dr. Griffin, an outstanding pastor and leader in race relations." (Dr. Griffin was elected First Vice-president of the Baptist General Convention of Texas in 1996.)

The class was a highlight for many reasons, not the least of which was its broadening effect on the perspective of the teachers.

The year also held responsibilities on the national level for Eula Mae. Mrs. George R. Martin, national WMU President, had asked her to serve as chairman of the Program Committee for the Week of Prayer for Home Missions for 1956, and to serve on the Allocations Committee for the Annie Armstrong Offering. At that time, and up until the early 1960s, the WMU, SBC Executive Board was involved in determining both the Lottie Moon and Annie Armstrong allocations.[3]

"I think all of us felt the responsibility quite keenly," Eula Mae said later. "It was true then, as it is now, that there were more requests than money to fund them. It made for some hard decisions."

When 1955 drew to a close, it marked not only the end of a gloriously successful Diamond Jubilee year, but also the end of Mrs. Mathis's six-year tenure, and the election of Ethel (Mrs. Clem) Hardy as President. A former missionary to Brazil and a strong speaker, Mrs. Hardy was also a graduate of Central Texas Baptist Sanitarium (now Hillcrest Baptist Hospital) School of Professional Nursing. Her years in Brazil

SPECIAL OCCASION—Dr. A. Hope Owen, president of Wayland Baptist College (later University) joins Eula Mae (second from left) and two of "her presidents" at a reception following Wayland's awarding of an honorary doctorate to Eula Mae in August, 1956. Marie Mathis (second from right) led Texas WMU from 1949 to 1955, and Ethel Hardy (extreme right) from 1955 to 1961.

had been highlighted by work with orphaned and neglected children.

Although the Diamond Jubilee year was over, there were still diamonds in the picture. Millie Morton announced plans to marry Ivyloy Bishop, former national Director of Royal Ambassadors, and now a professor at Wayland Baptist College (later University).

The couple was married December 18 at First Baptist Church in New Orleans, with Eula Mae as maid of honor and Mrs. Mathis serving as mother of the bride. Mary Lee Vines (Miller), BSU city-wide director in Houston, was a bridesmaid; David Mein, missionary to Brazil, was best man, and Glendon McCullough, then with the Home Mission Board, a groomsman. Also participating in the ceremony were June Cooper, later a missionary to Japan, and Monte McMahan (Clendinning), subsequently a missionary and later associated with the World Missions Center at Southwestern Seminary. J. D. Grey, former President of the Southern Baptist Convention, conducted the ceremony. Alma Hunt and Juliette Mather attended from WMU, SBC.

Later, Eula Mae would recite the list and then add, "I think you could say it was a denominational wedding!"

The year 1956 brought a major change to Texas WMU when the program staff tripled. The position of Young People's Secretary, which had included YWA, GA, and Sunbeams, was divided into three positions. In March, Amelia Morton Bishop was named part-time YWA director and Dollie Culp, part-time GA director. A few months later, Joyce Gill (Kelsey) was elected to lead the Sunbeam work.

THIS I REMEMBER: Eula Mae, who was "Aunt Judy" to our family, was a presence in our children's lives from the very beginning—literally!

Danny was born January 11, 1957, and Judy Lee on July 17, l959; she was named for Eula Mae and for Mary Lee Vines (Miller) a dear friend in BSU work. Later, with Aunt Judy's permission, our daughter changed the spelling on her given name to "Judi."

Aunt Judy made it a point to be in Plainview at the birth of each child. Then, after I had come home from the hospital, she took a week's vacation and came to take care of us.

It started out rather precariously, but in each case she and the baby involved learned together, and she was a decided help. When it was time for Danny and me to come home from the hospital, Ivyloy and Aunt Judy came to get us. My husband was driving; the hospital nurse opened the front door, and I sat beside him. Then the nurse opened the back door where Aunt Judy sat, sticking out her arms like two rigid poles to receive the baby. The nurse hesitated, then slowly handed Danny to her, murmuring encouragement, "Hold him close; he won't break."

Aunt Judy relaxed and cuddled the baby. It was a new day. By the time Judy Lee arrived, Aunt Judy was an "old hand."

—Millie Bishop

Royal Ambassadors, which had been under the WMU umbrella, had been moved to the Brotherhood Department. The Southern Baptist Convention in 1954 voted that this changeover be made, with a three-year transition period indicated. Robert Chapman, whose work in Texas had been co-sponsored by WMU and Brotherhood, moved into the Brotherhood offices in late 1954.

"That was a traumatic time for us," Eula Mae said. "Robert Chapman had been a part of our WMU family and a good worker. To have him leave, to lose an organization like RAs was quite a change. And yet, we recognized at the time that it was really better for the boys to have men working with them in their missions organization. They needed role models, and this provided them. It was hard, but it was right."

One 1956 event which Eula Mae much appreciated but seldom mentioned in public came about when Wayland Baptist College (now University) conferred on her the honorary Doctor of Laws degree. The event took place in conjunction with the August commencement, with A. Hope Owen, president of Wayland, presiding. Among those present were Eula Mae's sister, Erma Barnett; her mother, Mrs. Alice Henderson; along with Mrs. Mathis, then immediate past president of Texas WMU; Mrs Clem Hardy, then current president; Mrs. Henry Heck of Plainview, WMU president of district nine who later served as Recording Secretary for Texas WMU; and Dr. and Mrs. Ivyloy Bishop, also of Plainview.

How did Eula Mae feel about all this?

"I was overwhelmed," she said. "I couldn't believe it was happening to me. I did not think I was at all qualified to receive such an honor. Then, as I thought about it, I realized it came to me through WMU, and it was really a tribute to our organization, not just to me. This I very much appreciated. The hard part was getting together a message which might in some measure do justice to the occasion."

As those who were present would attest, this she did, and did it with distinction.

A parallel honor came in 1970 when Mary Hardin-Baylor College (later University) awarded her the honorary Doctor of Humanities.

One of the most significant programs to begin in the mid-1950s was what was initially called the Latin American Scholarships, providing financial help to qualified Hispanic students. Funds came from the Mary Hill Davis Offering for State Missions.

"When the program was started," Eula Mae said, "we had very few applicants to apply for a scholarship to one of our Baptist schools, but that has changed through the years. It has been a joy and an inspiration to meet with worthy, outstanding young people who want an education, who want to go to a Baptist college."

At that time, applicants would come to the Baptist Building for an interview after they had been recommended, and after files and transcripts had been checked. Meeting with them would be leadership of WMU, State Missions Commission, and other staffers in the state convention. As the number of applicants grew, each then met with a sub-committee or small group so that the interview could be personalized. Subsequently, all applicants and BGCT workers were together in a larger meeting, followed by lunch.

The first chairman of the Latin American Scholarship Committee was J. Woodrow Fuller, who headed the Missions Division of the State Missions Commission. He was followed by Charles McLaughlin, and later Charles Lee Williamson, who were the three chairmen with whom Eula Mae worked in this capacity during her tenure.

"To me, these meetings with scholarship applicants were so exciting that I found myself wishing all Texas Baptists could see and hear these young people," Eula Mae later said. "When we got together for the luncheon which concluded the meeting, we would invite all the Latin American staff in the Baptist Building to attend. It helped our applicants to see that we have professionals here in BGCT who are Latin American and speak two languages.

"In more recent years, the program has been broadened to include a Black scholarship program."[4] In the 1980s scholarships were made available to Asians and the deaf.

"I believe this scholarship effort has proved to be one of the great investments that we as Texas Baptists have made in people. We are aware of its long-reaching effects when we see where some of these scholarship recipients are today, and the leadership they have given to Texas Baptist churches and Texas Baptist work."

In the overall picture, WMU work among the Latin Americans throughout the state blossomed in the late 1950s. President Ethel Hardy, in her days as a missionary in Brazil, had related well to the South American women, and that emphasis carried over into her work with Hispanics in Texas. Certainly the work was not new; the Hispanic WMU had been organized in 1917,[5] and WMU through the years had lent a helping hand. Eula Mae had been involved in it, in one way or another, since her days as Young People's Secretary in 1946-47.

Names prominent during the early years, many of whom Eula Mae had known and worked with, included Adelina García, Esther Moye, Martha Thomas Ellis, Esperanza Ramírez, Noemí Cuevas (Jiménez), Frances Salazar, Irene Parades, Mary Godsey, and Gregoria González. Also active in the work were Rebecca Aguirre, Raquel Mireles, Isabel Estrada, Virginia Vela, Francisca Chapoy (Flores), and Berta Montero, among others.

In the late 1950s and early 1960s, materials in Spanish flourished. *Nuestra Tarea*, the Spanish version of *Royal Service*, made its appearance, as did leader manuals. Biographical leaflets of missions leaders and "How to Organize" brochures were also introduced.

The relationship between Texas WMU and the Hispanic organization was described as a close one. Noemí Cuevas came to work in 1959 as a Home Mission Board Field Worker in the State Missions Commission offices, working with the Hispanic WMU. Subsequently she became Language Consultant for Texas WMU in 1965 and served until 1968, when she married Manuel Jiménez. It was during that period that Texas WMU set up the plan whereby two Hispanic women would be members-at-large of the WMU Executive Board.

THIS I REMEMBER: During my lifetime, God has given me the privilege of working with some wonderful Christians from whom I learned much. Looking back, I would say that no one helped me more than Eula Mae.

I had known her even before I went to the Baptist Building in 1959. She expected those who worked with her to be prepared for their task or assignment, to present it effectively, and to be dressed in a manner appropriate for the occasion. Yes, she had high expectations, but then she expected no less from herself. Her commitment to her work was matched by her concern for individuals—she really cared. We felt this, and because we did, we wanted to live up to her expectations. I tried hard to emulate her, knowing it would help me to reach more of our Spanish-speaking churches. I benefitted much from her leadership.

—Noemí Cuevas Jiménez

Eula Mae would point out on occasion that the Hispanic women continue to have their own organization, but that they are also a part of Texas WMU. "Their leadership serves on the Executive Board," she would explain. "We help them with leadership training and provide financial assistance." Later, in the early 1960s, the relationship became even closer when unification of the Mexican Baptist Convention with the BGCT began in 1961 and was completed in 1964.[6] Hispanics in Texas became a part of BGCT, but also maintained their own identity, conducted their own convention, held associational meetings, and published their own newspaper.

Meanwhile, far to the north, seeds were being planted in the Minnesota-Wisconsin area that would impact Eula Mae and Texas WMU, as well as the Baptist General Convention of Texas. In the 1950s, several Texans from the Lubbock area found themselves "up north," and could not locate a Southern Baptist church in their vicinity. They called Ralph Grant, then pastor of First Baptist Church in Lubbock.

"We can't find a church," they said unhappily.

After a pause, the response came, "Well, start one!"

Startled at first, they decided to act upon his suggestion.

Thus it was that in 1956 seven Southern Baptist congregations in Minnesota and Wisconsin invited the BGCT to join them in reaching persons for Christ. The state convention accepted, and was joined by the Home Mission Board in the endeavor.[7] Texas WMU very quickly became involved in what was to be a memorable adventure. The women responded enthusiastically to the needs in what came to be called "our northern-most association." Before long, teams of workers were journeying to the Minnesota-Wisconsin area to help with leadership training. Texas WMU brought key Minnesota-Wisconsin workers to the Texas WMU House Party at Baylor University, both to broaden their understanding of the work, and to enable Texas women to hear about this area of home missions. The Pastors and Wives Retreat came into being, funded by the Mary Hill Davis Offering. Held at Green Lakes Conference Center, this annual event was made possible for all Southern Baptist pastors and wives in that area to have a "getaway weekend." The programs were both inspirational and informative, with a good amount of fellowship time provided. Leaders from Texas WMU and the BGCT State Missions Commission went each year for the occasion. Usually this included Eula Mae and the state WMU president, along with State Missions Commission leadership such as Charles McLaughlin, Charles Lee Williamson, Eugene Greer, and others. The event has become a much-anticipated, cherished tradition.

Through the years a close bond developed between the two groups. During Eula Mae's tenure, Texas leadership worked initially with Frank Burress and Warren Littleford, then with Otha Winningham. In 1981, the Minnesota-Wisconsin team was strengthened by the addition of Betty Lynn Cadle as Director of WMU/Christian Social Ministries. Minnesota-Wisconsin became a fellowship in 1974 and a convention in 1983, but maintained ties with Texas. In 1993 native Texan William Tinsley became Executive Director of the Minnesota-Wisconsin Baptist Convention.

THIS I REMEMBER: *Some people touch our lives in especially meaningful ways. For me, Eula Mae Henderson was one of these. I first met her in January 1963, when I was the new YWA Director for Georgia WMU, and I remember what an encourager she was for new workers.*

Today, I appreciate her for other reasons as well. Since I came to the Minnesota-Wisconsin staff in 1981, I have seen the evidence of her care and concern stamped all over Minnesota-Wisconsin Baptist history. In 1956, when Minnesota-Wisconsin was accepted into fellowship with the BGCT, she was a pivotal figure in leading out in the training of new churches. That continued on through the years. Since 1976, the women of Minnesota-Wisconsin have led their own conferences, with assistance as needed from Texas WMU.

And then there is the annual Pastors-Wives Retreat, begun while Eula Mae was Executive Director, and made possible by the Mary Hill Davis Offering. Without doubt, this event makes a decided impact in the lives of the couples who come, and in their churches.

It is said that "One woman can make a difference."
Eula Mae did. Her influence still does.
   —Betty Lynn Cadle

The banner year 1956—in which 79 percent of all Texas Baptist churches had a missions organization of some kind[8] and the Standard of Excellence was replaced by Aims for Advancement as the plan of work—gave way to an equally eventful 1957. Elaine Dickson, a Southwestern Seminary student, became part-time YWA Secretary, serving for a year before accepting a position with WMU, SBC. Dollie Culp, who had been part-time in GA work, became full-time. On the national level, the Ministerial Relief Offering, which had been a part of the national program for so many years, was to be dropped after 1957 at the suggestion of the Finance Committee of the Southern Baptist Convention Executive Committee.[10] The Relief and Annuity Board would assume care for all beneficiaries, thus eliminating one of Texas WMU's prayer days and offerings.

On the state level, the BGCT Executive Board voted to begin the 1958 convention on Monday with no other convention meetings immediately preceding. Consequently, in the next two years, WMU held Annual Meetings in the spring, the first in San Angelo, and the second in Galveston. In 1960, the BGCT reverted to the original plan in order to sustain attendance at the general convention.

In 1959, Eula Mae rejoiced to have a full staff again. Joy Phillips came to be GA Director when Dollie Culp joined the staff of First Baptist Church, Dallas. Mary Jane Nethery arrived to lead the YWA program.

Joy, her interest in missions quickened by the YWA House Party she had attended, had returned from that event to become a GA leader in her church and in the association. In her own words, "Dollie Culp saw something in me, and gave me opportunities to grow." When the GA position was vacant, Joy, who planned to enroll in seminary in the fall, was asked to come on an interim basis. The summer of 1969 was looming and GA camps crowded the calendar. "I am amazed at the confidence that Dollie and Eula Mae placed in me," Joy said later. "There was never a greener leader anywhere—never!"

Interestingly enough, she expressed the same feelings that Eula Mae had mentioned when she came to the state office in the 1940s: "I don't know much about state work at all, but I have the confidence I can learn."

And she did. The interim position became permanent.

Mary Jane Nethery, who was to spend six years leading the Texas YWA program, had first encountered Eula Mae as a student at Southwestern Seminary, and later at state YWA House Parties when she brought groups of student nurses to attend the Belton events. She described EMH as "attractive and almost regal in appearance, yet thoroughly approachable. She was warm and friendly; in fact, she was quite an encourager, and that made it easy for me to fit in."

Mary Jane's experience her first day at work seemed to follow a pattern expressed by several incoming staffers. Eula Mae would stop what she was doing when the new staff member arrived and invite the fledgling worker into her office, tastefully furnished with pictures and artifacts from different parts of the world. Then, after suggesting that the newcomer sit down, she would draw up a chair beside her rather than resume her place behind her desk. And they would talk.

It made for a good beginning.

Joyce Gill, at this point, was experienced at state work, having come two years earlier. She had learned many things, including Eula Mae's commitment to work. Rather ruefully, she told the story of an arduous series of workshops, after which she and Eula Mae arrived back in Dallas. Too tired to cook, they decided to pick up hamburgers and take them to Joyce's house, just up the street from where Eula Mae lived. This they did, flopping into the chairs in Joyce's dining room. Getting out their food, they prepared to eat and Eula Mae led the blessing. In it, she thanked the Lord for the work done and asked His help in the labors that lay ahead. Without thinking, Joyce blurted out, "I like to work too, but couldn't we just eat before we work some more?"

As the decade drew to a close, literacy workshops were a vital part of the community missions program. Long interested in literacy, Eula Mae carved out time from her schedule to teach a young man in Dallas to read, and brought to the office updates on his progress—and hers. In midsummer, she reported that he could read fifth and sixth grade material, and then commented, "Dallas County had approximately 30,000 illiterates. Now it has only 29,999!"

6

On the Road, Onstage, Backstage

"Ten of the seventeen district workshops are history! The nine members of the traveling team came through with flying colors, partly because of nylon jersey dresses! But the real success of those meetings was due to the enthusiastic response from our district and associational leadership. We are grateful for all of you who made such specific efforts to get 'your' people there."

Writing to board members on April 25, 1962, the Executive Secretary-Treasurer leaned toward her typewriter, reading what she had written. Her dark curly hair was now decidedly tinged with gray, but her brown eyes still radiated the same joy in her work that had characterized her these 15 years in state WMU work.

The second series of workshops was scheduled for one week later. In the same letter, she went on to tell what she and the other state leadership would be doing during the intervening week. Special events were planned for every age level. President Leila (Mrs. Bert) Black would be in the district two retreat and the district ten House Party; Joyce Gill was slated for the Dallas Association House Party; Joy Phillips was busy with GA Galaxy correspondence and coronation service preparations; Mary Jane Nethery was promoting the YWA train trip to Ridgecrest, as well as helping college and hospital YWAs; Eula Mae would be in the district twelve retreat.

Then, with tongue-in-cheek, Eula Mae added, "And for

those of you who may have any spare time, there's always the rings in the prayer charts!"[1]

The charts were being prepared for the upcoming seventy-fifth anniversary of WMU, SBC under the direction of State Prayer Chairman Dora Jean (Mrs. Matthew) Sanderford, a former missionary to Uruguay. She was then serving with her husband at the Baptist Spanish Publishing House in El Paso. The charts were held together with rings, and were to be used beginning July 18. All available hands were needed to "ring them."

On the day that the letter was written, much was going on in the state WMU office as well. Mrs. Black was in Dallas for a committee meeting regarding the Japan New Life Crusade. In the weekly prayer meeting held the day before in the Baptist Building, BGCT leadership such as T. A. Patterson and C. Wade Freeman had spoken about the tremendous opportunities in Japan. "I wish you could have heard them," Eula Mae said. "Dr. Freeman referred to Dr. Patterson as a missionary statesman." And then she added, "Certainly we are fortunate in Texas to have such leadership!"

Such were the times in the spring of 1962. The decade brought many new opportunities, but it had begun with unforeseen setbacks: a "medical slowdown" on Eula Mae's part in 1960, the death of her father in 1961, and then, on the office front, the minor matter of moving into a new office without missing a step—especially when some of the new chairs had not arrived.

As the decade had begun, and after months of preparation, EMH was poised to take off on a mission trip to the Orient. Her companion was to be Edna Frances Dawkins of the Foreign Mission Board, and both were excited about their itinerary and the missionaries they would visit on their journeys. Eula Mae, whose health was ordinarily excellent, had not been feeling well, and went for her annual check-up. Her fears were confirmed when the problem was diagnosed as hepatitis. She was told that she must have bed rest for two or three weeks, and then only limited activity for a few more. Obviously, she could not make the trip and was profoundly disappointed. For so many months, she had looked forward to seeing the work and being with missionaries, and had been so pleased that she would be traveling with Edna Frances. Now Edna Frances would have to make alternate plans. All in all, it was a major disappointment. However, she accepted the medical verdict and, assisted by family, friends, and staff, set about following the road to recovery. When asked about her progress during these weeks, she would say, "I live on tough street—and I live in the last house!"

Later, she would talk about how "God had used the time for good," and, holding up her Bible, make the comment, "This book is even more precious to me than ever."

The year 1961 brought both shock and sadness into Eula Mae's life when her father passed away suddenly. Rex and Alice Henderson had continued to live in Oklahoma City, as did Eula Mae's sister, Erma Barnett. In the fall, as the Annual Meeting was about to begin in Austin, word came of Rex Henderson's death, which cast a somber note over the proceedings. Eula Mae flew home and remained with her mother and sister for several days. Friends from Texas went to be with them.

Rex Henderson was a decided influence on the lives of both his daughters. The priority he set on being a Christian and living the Christian life, his example of unswerving faithfulness to his church, and his high standards and diligence in fulfilling everyday responsibilities in the workplace, made lifelong imprints on both Eula Mae and Erma.

And then there was the challenge of the "chairs that weren't."

Early in the decade, the Texas WMU office moved from the third floor of the Baptist Building upstairs to Suite 409, opting to change a part of the furniture in the process. Move time came; the new chairs for the reception area did not. However, when Eula Mae wrote her midspring letter she took the positive approach. Yes, she pointed out, the new chairs would be here in about a month. In the meantime, of course there were some furnishings on hand. "We do have a new electric typewriter, a seat for two people, and a step table in our reception room!" Certainly "flexibility" and "adaptability" were key words in the WMU vocabulary even then.

Eula Mae had one more "moving challenge" in 1977 when the WMU office was relocated to Suite 102 in the Baptist Building. Some observer commented at the time that "challenge" was simply the religious term for "problem."

The 1961 Annual Meeting marked the end of Ethel Hardy's tenure, the presidency being limited at that time to no more than six consecutive one-year terms. Mrs. Hardy was a strong speaker, and one whose ongoing commitment to missions could never be questioned. She displayed on the home front the same total dedication that had characterized her mission service in Brazil.

Leila Black of Crosbyton was then named state President, the eighth woman to hold that position. Eula Mae had worked with her when Mrs. Black served on local, associational, and district levels. For five years preceding her election to state leadership, "the lady from Crosbyton" had been President of district nine WMU and, by virtue of this office, a Vice-President of the state organization. She was tall and attractive, and "knew WMU from the grass roots up." She began her labors on the state level with the same dedication and diligence that had characterized her earlier endeavors.

Through the years, Eula Mae's work was a balance between time spent in the office, and time on the field; always there seemed to be a pull in two directions. She also strove for balance between foreign, home, state, and associational missions, although her work in the first three areas seemed to garner more publicity. To stay abreast of work being done in the varied areas, she often took short but well-planned visits to mission fields, such as the one she took in June 1962. Frequently these were made in conjunction with a state, national, or international meeting. This one was no exception. She went to the Annual Meeting of WMU, SBC in San Francisco, going early to participate in a prayer retreat, to be followed by a missions tour in the area. Both were choice. At the retreat, Bertha Smith, a Southern Baptist missionary noted for her service in China and Taiwan, shared prayer experiences "as only she could do." After the meeting, Jack Combes, Director of Language Missions in California, arranged for tours in San Francisco.

"We saw firsthand many of our home missionaries on their field of service," Eula Mae said upon her return, "Paul Rogosin and the Slavic Baptist Church, Peter Chen and the Chinese church, and several Latin American and Indian churches."[2]

Often after such sessions the report came back from those she visited, and those accompanying her: "Eula Mae loves missionaries, and it showed!"

That particular Annual Meeting, although outstanding in programming, also had a touch of sadness. Mildred (Mrs.

William) McMurry who had led so capably in many WMU, SBC areas of work—she was probably best known for mission study—was retiring in November. However, as Texans were happy to note, she would be at the Texas WMU Annual Meeting in November.

"Mrs. Mac," as she was sometimes called, was one of EMH's favorites. Eula Mae spoke several times of a message she heard "Mrs. Mac" deliver at Glorieta. "She was encouraging us to put more effort into our mission study, more time in preparation, more creative ways of presentation," Eula Mae recalled. "Then, as she concluded her challenge, her words were 'Put aside your flickering candle of feeble preparation, for in the atomic age, the world is lit by lightning!' And she sat down. I was glad I was already sitting because I was so impressed by what she said, and the way she said it, I just had to sit there and think a while."

THIS I REMEMBER: The first time that I was President of San Saba Association WMU in the 1960s, our second child was born one week before the House Party at Baylor. At that time the WMU Executive Board met just prior to House Party and I knew that with a one-week old baby girl, I would be unable to attend. I wrote Miss Henderson and explained I could not be at the meeting since Donna had just been born.

By return mail, a letter came to Donna from Miss Henderson, to welcome our little girl into the world. The letter talked about this big, wonderful planet that God had made, and went on to tell Donna briefly that the writer hoped Donna would get to know God some day. It was a precious letter to a one-week-old baby girl.

At that time I wondered how a woman as busy as Miss Henderson, one week before the House Party, would have the time to write a letter to a baby girl. However, this was the kind of person that Eula Mae Henderson was. She had time for everyone. She cared.
        —Annette Reid

After months of planning, mountains of correspondence, countless committee meetings, and more than one trip to San Antonio, the GA Galaxy was held at the San Antonio Municipal Auditorium in the summer of 1962. Texas GA Director Joy Phillips was in charge, but in an event of this size, the entire state WMU staff was involved.

More than 6,000 girls attended the Galaxy, which was staged to celebrate the fiftieth anniversary of Girls' Auxiliary coming up in 1963. It was the largest WMU gathering held in

Texas in 82 years.³ Three national gatherings were subsequently held in Memphis, Tennessee the next year to climax the observance. Joy sponsored a group of more than 2,000 Texas GAs to one of these sessions.

Eula Mae, who had been in on the planning of the GA event from the beginning, was exuberant in describing the Texas meeting. "It was a real joy to see our Joy at the Galaxy. For months she had done excellent planning and preparation. Mrs. Otto Dukes, president of San Antonio WMU, proved to be a real standby through planning, registration, and in the Galaxy itself.

"Unless you were there for the autograph party, you do not know what it is like to be so popular with so many GAs. One girl was reported to have Joy Phillips' autograph six times, and another said she would trade three Joy Phillips for one Mickey Mantle!"⁴ So much for fame!

Meanwhile, that same summer, the almost 200 Texas YWAs at Ridgecrest were also in the spotlight, receiving several honors. For one of these, the group received an athletic trophy—three tin cans, graduated in size, with appropriate wording—which Texas YWA Director Mary Jane Nethery kept in her office for several months.

And language missions was not to be outdone! Martha Thomas Ellis and Noemí Cuevas, both experienced workers with Hispanics, did a series of workshops across Texas—21 of them.

The year climaxed with a trip to Minnesota-Wisconsin, the "northern-most association" as it was then called. Working with Mrs. Kenneth King, Associational WMU President, Texas WMUers went north to "take our sisters a mini-House Party" by doing leadership training in five different areas. Eula Mae reported that the group was "welcomed not only by our Baptist people, but also by the trees, lovely in their thrilling autumn colors!" As Mary Lee (Mrs. Howard) Bennett, state Stewardship Chairman and a member of the group commented, "We ran out of ooh's and ah's, and had to send back to Texas for some more!"

Eula Mae went on to describe the foliage in detail, commenting on the various shades of gold, orange, red, and green.

REMEMBER WHEN—
Attired in Indonesian saris at the Texas WMU House Party in 1963, Eula Mae and her fourth president, Leila Black (1961-63), share some of the highlights of a trip to the Orient with an after-session group.

Then she added, "We saw a great deal of beauty, but we also saw dedication and love for our Baptist churches there. The churches are not large in membership, but they are large in spirit and purpose."[5]

The Texas WMU Annual Meeting for the Jubilee Year of WMU, SBC (1963) was done in the spectacular fashion that often characterized the multi-day conventions in city auditoriums with adequate staging facilities. That year it was San Antonio. The theme selected, "Freedom's Holy Light," was carried out in messages, music, and dramas. Even the attire worn by the ushers was colorfully thematic: blue skirts, white blouses, red weskits. Additionally, the ushers carried hand-size Jubilee torches emblazoned with the word "QUIET!"

Minutes for the opening session relate that "Against a dark blue background a 14' x 16' flat stood on a revolving stage in the middle of the platform. The theme 'Freedom's Holy Light' was reflected across the gold background with a Jubilee torch upon it. Above the stage setting was a bronze eagle. Red, white, and blue bunting draped each side.

"The auditorium was darkened, and the stage setting spotlighted as Mrs. Woodson Armes of Fort Worth brought the Call to Worship. After developing the concept 'Ye shall know the truth, and the truth shall make you free,' she gave a brief biography of one of the great women who was a torchbearer for liberty in Christ. As she spoke of Mary Hill Davis, the stage revolved to reveal a living portrait of Mrs. Davis, portrayed by Mrs. R. L. Brown of College Station."[6]

The meeting was off to a good start. Such elaborate staging was enjoyed and appreciated by the women in that era before spectaculars became the norm. At the same time, attention to details brought about some interesting moments.

Dollie Culp, who had returned to the state WMU office in 1960 as office manager, oftimes had the privilege of adding stage manager for state meetings to her list of responsibilities.

She related an incident that happened in south Texas, one in which a men's hockey team was using a part of the same coliseum-complex as WMU. The Annual Meeting session had started and Dollie, backstage, was keeping her eyes glued on Eula Mae, who was seated on the stage. A look, or a nod, from EMH would tell Dollie that something was amiss which needed to be corrected.

On this occasion, the nod told her that the unusually loud male voices coming from one end of the convention center were drifting onto the stage, and interfering with the program. Dollie hurried in the direction of the noise. It turned out to be a men's locker room, where a leading hockey team was "whooping it up." An assistant stage manager told her there was nothing she could do to quiet them. Dollie tried several times to get the attention of the noisy players through the door, but the din continued.

"Then," she determined, "there was only one thing left to do. I opened the door and went in. The noise, so ear-splitting earlier, stopped abruptly. The silence was deafening.

"I never told Miss Henderson what I saw in that room. I never intend to! But the problem was solved."[7]

THIS I REMEMBER: When our children were both preschoolers in Plainview, Ivyloy and I had a two-week stint in the Dallas area while he served as camp pastor at a nearby encampment. In between the two weeks, we needed to return to Plainview for a wedding.

Eula Mae ("Aunt Judy") offered to keep the two children during our hurried trip. I remember asking, "Are you sure?" And she had replied confidently, "Of course!"

Ivyloy and I returned to Dallas late Sunday night to find the children in bed, and a rather harried-looking Aunt Judy.

"How did it go?" I inquired.

She took a deep breath. "I'm glad I did it, but you didn't tell me everything. The hardest part was this morning, trying to get to Sunday School and church. You didn't mention the hassles in the bathroom, or that one child gets dirty all over again while you're dressing the other one. You didn't talk about misplaced Bibles or hair ribbons or leather belts. I did remember to stuff my purse with crackers." She sighed, and then added grimly, "I am writing the Sunday School Board tomorrow! From now on, any mother with small children doesn't have to worry about whether she can mark down ON TIME or BROUGHT BIBLE or OFFERING or anything! If she just gets there, she's 100 percent!"

—Millie Bishop

In December of 1963 Eula Mae found herself in an unparalleled situation when Leila Black had to resign the state presidency. She had been having eye problems for several months and they became increasingly acute. Her doctors strongly advised her to give up the work to preserve her eyesight. She did so, with much regret.

"I wish I could tell you what it has meant to me to serve as President of Texas WMU these two years," she wrote. "A woman could not have had nor asked for a greater opportunity of service. I wish there were words to express my sincere appreciation for the relationships we have had, the experiences we have shared, the opportunities we have met. All have been blessings in my life, and are moments I shall never forget."[8]

Following the Texas WMU bylaws dealing with such an emergency, Virginia (Mrs. Tom) Drewett, Recording Secretary, called a meeting of the Executive Board early in January of 1964. The board voted to ask four vice-presidents to assume the major responsibilities of the president until a new leader could be elected at the next Annual Meeting in the fall. Selected were Mrs. I. E. Lamberth, Tyler; Mrs. Joe T. King, Childress; Mrs. R. L. Brown, College Station; and Mrs. H. C. Hunt, Gregory.

Each was given specific responsibilities, and Eula Mae worked with the individual vice-presidents in the assigned areas. Thus the unusual year passed.

Ophelia (Mrs. C. J.) Humphrey was elected president at the Annual Meeting in the fall of 1964, bringing to the position an impressive combination of youthful energy, experience, and missions vision. Like many of her predecessors, she had a multi-level WMU background, to which she had added the firsthand knowledge gained from several mission trips abroad. Her husband, C. J., shared her missions commitment; in fact, he had served as president of the district ten Brotherhood while Ophelia was president of the district WMU. Later, C. J. was Texas Brotherhood President. The couple lived in Amarillo.

Mrs. Humphrey was the first president to serve a four-year tenure, the Texas WMU bylaws having changed the length of presidential service from six years to four. Like several of her predecessors, she had a burden for the Hispanic work in Texas, and favored changing the location of Hispanic WMU work from the Language Missions Department to Texas WMU. Additionally, she played a dominant role three years later in developing the Texas Baptist River Ministry. Her understand-

SIGNS OF THE TIMES—Hats were "definitely in" at the Texas WMU Annual Meeting in Houston, Texas, in 1965. Eula Mae and her fifth president, Ophelia Humphrey, pause for a moment just after Mrs. Humphrey had been re-elected. She served from 1964 to 1968.

ing of WMU was reflected in her philosophy, "Each church has its own distinct personality and needs. Our need in WMU is to be flexible enough to permit each church to work out its own strong missions education program."⁹

Another 1964 standout for Eula Mae involved three things very meaningful to her: Corpus Christi, the people of district five, and a WMU pin.

Apparently the pin had been given by the Texas WMU in

the early 1950s to Estelle (Mrs. A. A.) Cummins, then president of the district, in recognition for 100 percent reporting. She wore it until the end of her tenure, then presented it to her successor, Cleo (Mrs. Ernest) Pierce.

"She charged me to wear it with honor," Mrs. Pierce said, "and to keep district five not only 100 percent in reporting, but also a Standard district, as she had done. It was my privilege five years later to pass it on to Barbara (Mrs. Grady) West with the same charge and the same achievements, unblemished."

Mrs. West then pinned it on Mauriece (Mrs. Earl) Johnston at the end of a five-year tenure, with the honors it represented still intact. Mrs. Johnston moved to San Antonio during the second year of her term of office, and the plan of reporting changed. However, the pin was passed on to Inez (Mrs. H. C.) Hunt who was charged with continuing the honored tradition. This she did.

Then, as the district plan was discontinued in Texas in 1964, the question came up: what to do with the pin since it no longer belonged to any one particular person?

The answer was unanimous. "Let's give it back to the one who first gave it to us!"

Thus, at the Annual Meeting held that year in Corpus Christi, Mrs. Pierce called Eula Mae to the platform. "I am happy to have the privilege of presenting this district five pin to our District Five Scholarship Girl, Eula Mae Henderson. We are right proud of the way you turned out! Eula Mae, I pin this on you in recognition of your 17 years of 100 percent leadership in Texas, and charge you to continue!"[10]

It was a high moment for the "District Five Scholarship Girl," and a tribute she never forgot.

In mid- and late-1960, another side of Eula Mae was blossoming, and one that had no relationship to Texas WMU. She had become an avid football fan—if the Dallas Cowboys or the University of Oklahoma were playing.

"We would watch some of those games on television," reported Katharine Bryan, who joined the Texas WMU staff in 1965, "and if a poor play was committed, EMH would kick off her shoes and protest loudly to the TV screen."[11]

Katharine had followed Mary Jane Nethery as YWA Director when the latter became Dean of Women at Mary Hardin-Baylor College. (Later, Mary Jane became Executive Director of Tennessee WMU.)

Katharine had come to Texas WMU from WMU, SBC where she had been Promotional Associate in the GA Department. A graduate of Southwestern Seminary, she had attended several Texas YWA and GA events. She was to be with Texas WMU until 1977, combining her YWA work with GA work part of the time. She then became Baptist Young Women's Director the last seven years of her tenure; a part of this time she also directed the Baptist Women's program. (Later, Katharine returned to her native state and became Executive Director of Tennessee WMU.)

Another addition to the Texas WMU staff in 1965 was Noemí Cuevas, who became Language Missions Director, moving from the BGCT State Missions Commission. She promptly made plans to conduct the first WMU conference in Spanish at the WMU House Party that summer; both Mrs. Humphrey and Eula Mae were delighted.

Eula Mae was seldom caught speechless, but Joy Phillips learned from personal experience that it could indeed happen.

"I went to her in 1966 to tell her that I was going to marry Charlie Fenner and go to Japan as a missionary," Joy related. "Eula Mae was at a complete loss for words, a phenomenon which I never saw before or since! This happened just before the YWA House Party at Mary Hardin-Baylor, so

Eula Mae officially announced my engagement during a gathering of the program personnel there on campus. In typical EMH fashion, she made it a big occasion by ordering a cake, complete with bride and groom. Then, since she was doing the Calls to Worship on Sunday morning she wove in something about the joy of following the Lord's leadership, even if it should lead to Japan. I was the first staff member to be appointed a missionary, and EMH came to our appointment service in Richmond."[12]

Before that event, Eula Mae took part in Joy and Charlie's wedding, writing and delivering a paraphrase of I Corinthians 13 as a part of the ceremony.

Years later, Eula Mae visited the Fenners in Japan when she led a mission tour to the Orient. On that occasion, speaking before the tour group as well as a group of her Japanese friends, Joy said "I stand before two groups: one a group of Japanese women who are my friends; the other the Henderson tour group from Texas, also my friends. I have one foot in Fukuoka, the other in Texas. One of my joys is to introduce people whom I love to each other, and in doing so, those people can communicate across cultural differences. For this concept of world missions, which came in part from my association with Miss Henderson, I am deeply and sincerely grateful."[13]

Further tributes came in the 1966 Annual Meeting, Eula Mae's twentieth anniversary in Texas WMU work. Unknown to her, President Ophelia Humphrey and others planned a special tribute involving several speakers and a brochure chronicling her 20 years of service. Written by Amelia Bishop, the brochure followed the acrostic "If You Are My Disciples." In addition to Mrs. Humphrey, speakers included Charles McLaughlin, Secretary of the State Missions Commission, who announced that the new chapel at the Mexican Baptist Bible Institute (later the Hispanic Baptist Seminary) in San Antonio would be named the Eula Mae Henderson Chapel. Others on the program were W. A. Criswell, Eula Mae's pastor who stressed her faithfulness to her church and her work for 20 years with 11-year-old juniors; T. A. Patterson, Executive Secretary of the Baptist General Convention of Texas; and Mrs. Robert Fling, longtime friend, former state Mission Study

Chairman, and in 1966 the President of national Woman's Missionary Union. Mrs. Humphrey, on behalf of Texas WMU, presented Eula Mae with a check for $2,500 with which to purchase a new car.

Eula Mae made a brief yet gracious response, although such attention usually embarrassed her. Each year, in her annual report, she strove to make sure the focus was on the work, not on her, as she reported on exceptional progress being made in local churches, and told how each had made giant steps forward.

"First Church, Petersburg . . .

"First Church, Schwab City . . .

"Lakeland Baptist Church, Lewisville . . .

"Central Baptist Church, San Antonio . . .

"First Latin Church, Sonora . . . "

Often, at such times, she would say, "This is not my report, but yours."

And it was.

7

Outreach, Inreach... Labor, Levity

"Oh, Lord! They have done so much with so little; and I have so much and I have done so little."

Thus Eula Mae Henderson prayed in 1967 when she toured the Rio Grande areas with a group for the first time, her head bowed, her dark hair now flecked with gray, and her brown eyes closed.

She had seen the river from two sides; she had met and talked with the people and had been in their small churches. She marveled at what they had accomplished with the little they had.

She was, in a word, overwhelmed.

What had prompted her visit? What lay in the background?

It had begun earlier that same year. A new chapter in missions history was unfolding.

Eula Mae and Ophelia Humphrey had been invited to the office of T. A. Patterson, Executive Secretary of the Baptist General Convention of Texas. Present also was Charles McLaughlin, Secretary of the State Missions Commission.

They had come together with a common interest, a common bond. Each had shown a strong interest in Hispanic work in Texas; each had manifested that interest by involvement in different areas of Latin American work. Each had been thinking "What else can we do?" Something more was obviously needed.

Dr. Patterson and Dr. McLaughlin shared their concerns which had been surfacing over a period of years, climaxing in a trip the two men and their wives had taken to the river in the fall of 1966. They described the lamentable conditions they found. They talked of the mounting needs, the increasing numbers of impoverished people lacking both spiritual and material resources. They spoke of the enormous expense involved in a project of this magnitude. Dr. McLaughlin mentioned a concept he had considered: established churches in Texas might adopt a portion of the territory along the river, and work with it as they would a mission in their own community. He stressed the importance of lay involvement.[1] One idea led to another. Mrs. Humphrey and Eula Mae listened with growing excitement.

The conference concluded with a significant question put to the two women. Would Texas WMU be willing to include an allocation for "work along the river" in the Mary Hill Davis Offering?

The women thought about this and prayed about it. They concluded that this project might well be something Texas WMU would want to undergird, but they needed more information before they discussed it with the WMU Executive Board.

Eula Mae realized she had been many times to towns and cities along the river, but had never actually toured the Rio Grande area itself. Traveling with Dr. McLaughlin, Eugene Greer, the Dallas Lees, and Huis Coy (Mrs. C.W., later Mrs. Elvis Egge), writer of the upcoming Week of Prayer for State Missions material, the Texas WMU leaders "saw with their own eyes and felt with their own hearts" both the deplorable conditions and the unlimited opportunities in the limitless miles along both sides of the Rio Grande.

They also came to understand something else—a feeling on the part of many border Hispanics that "the rest of Texas doesn't seem to know or care that we exist." As Mrs. Humphrey later described it, "We had to convince them that we did care, and that we meant business. We WILL do something, and quickly!"²

THIS I REMEMBER: One of my most treasured memories of Eula Mae happened on an early Rio Grande River trip. This was after Eula Mae, Charlie, and others made that initial trip, and before the famous "busload of women" trip.

This particular journey was a "first time" for Elmin Howell, who later became Director of the River Ministry work. In the group also were Eula Mae, Fred and Elizabeth Swank, Jay Skaggs, Mauriece Johnston, and Charlie and I.

The incident happened at Ojinaga. The pastor took us to a site where he wanted to build a church. Charlie looked around, then picked up a good-sized rock, and placed it on the site. Eula Mae then picked up two, and added them to Charlie's. We all followed suit as the Israelites had done after the Jordan was crossed.

Then Eula Mae placed her hand on the pile of stones, and all of us, one after another, added our hands to the pile. Looking down, Charlie said, "On this rock I will build my church," and then prayed, asking God to secure the site for a future church building.

I was standing next to Eula Mae and looked up at her as the prayer concluded. She was beaming with an inner joy that suffused her whole face. I have never forgotten that moment.

And yes—there is a church on that site today.
   —*Jewette McLaughlin*

Meetings with missionaries and moderators from associations bordering the Rio Grande followed, as did sessions with the Mexican Baptist leadership and the Southern Baptist Foreign Mission Board. Tours to the valley increased substantially.

In the spring, the executive boards of both the Baptist General Convention of Texas and Texas WMU endorsed the "Rio Grande Missions Thrust."[3] In the summer, it was promoted at the Texas WMU House Party.

The Week of Prayer for State Missions featured "the work along the river" as planned, but what happened next was assuredly unplanned.

"Beulah," one of the most violent hurricanes to hit Texas, roared across the Rio Grande Valley on September 20 of that year with winds up to 115 miles per hour, devastating everything in its wake. Torrential rains followed, pelting the area with from 10 to 30 inches. Some 300,000 persons in south Texas and Mexico were left homeless. Property damages were estimated at $100 million, with crop losses at $50 million.[4]

Texans swung into action. Hundreds went to the valley. Other hundreds in central Texas stayed home to minister to the hordes of people streaming upstate. Many associations throughout the state collected supplies to be sent to relief centers in the stricken area. Available buildings such as the old Valley Baptist Hospital building, vacant barracks, and a U.S. Army Air Force hanger, became warehouses, overseen by Bob Dixon, then Royal Ambassador Director for Texas Brotherhood.[5]

Texas WMUers were in the heart of the activity. As one woman put it, "We thought we'd be studying about the valley and sending in our offering. Instead, we're passing out food and clothing to the very people we've been studying about!"

And so the River Ministry, as it is known today, was born.

Eula Mae continued to make the work a priority, partnering not only with Dr. McLaughlin but also with Charles Lee Williamson who became Director of the Missions Division in 1968, and with Elmin Howell, who came that same year to head the River Ministry work. In retrospect, EMH made the comment, "Truly, I don't know of anything that has helped us as Texas Baptists as much as the River Ministry. We thought at first it would be for two or three years, and we were sincere in that; now we know it will go on until the Lord comes! As long as there are people along both sides of that river, there will be a need for ministry."[6]

The Annual Meeting of 1967 covered the same broad scope of missions typical of such sessions. Through the years, Eula Mae and the state presidents with whom she worked made every effort to include all aspects of mission work, as well as special features and outstanding music. Additionally, they incorporated some aspects of "everyday work" which could relate to all women. One segment of the 1967 meeting featured Eva Marie Kennard (later Mrs. Paul Dyke), who served in Berkeley, California and spoke on "The World at Our Door." She stressed the idea that "the internationals have come to our door—here by divine appointment. Often they are puzzled by our Christianity. Wouldn't it be wonderful if years later these internationals could say, 'When I was in America I went to the home of the Browns, or the Andersons, or the Smiths . . . and found Jesus there.'"

Lloyd Conner, pastor of First Baptist Church, Marfa, told how his people became involved with "The People of the River." "They said, 'Come over and help us. We want a church.' It was a small beginning. We met in the river bottom under the trees, but God blessed. The women began to make adobe bricks and stack them on the river bank. Many have been our experiences, but God's grace was always sufficient."[7]

Marge (Mrs. Charles) Caldwell told of her experiences in witnessing during a Dayton, Ohio meeting, indicating how her charm class gave her a chance to witness. Mrs. J. R. Lobaugh of Kansas City, WMU, SBC Recording Secretary, followed with a challenge for personal involvement in everyday witnessing opportunities.

A special feature came when Dr. and Mrs. O. K.

Armstrong, authors of *The Indomitable Baptists*, were introduced. The couple presented autographed copies of the book to Mrs. Humphrey and Eula Mae.

Music was led by Claude Rhea, with Earl Miller at the organ and Karen Carpenter (later Calhoun) at the piano. Both instrumentalists were familiar to the audience, having been a part of several Texas WMU events.

An important segment of the meeting, then as now, was the annual report brought by the Executive Secretary-Treasurer. Eula Mae, following a pattern that was her custom, referred in her printed report to the work of different churches—and one association—throughout the state. She called it "Echoes of Progress," and pointed out that "As I mention progress in one phase of our work, you may immediately echo a similar response in attainment in the church or association where you serve." Understandably, with the experiences along the river so much in her heart, she mentioned the Lower Rio Grande Association. "You would recognize this as a part of the section that suffered so much from the hurricane 'Beulah' the third week of September. The fourth week brought clean-up, and the close of another WMU year. With all their concern for cleaning houses, businesses, and churches; with locating people and working in relief centers, the presidents of every WMU in this association found time to see that reports reached their associational president, Mrs. J. A. Spradlin. The people could not come to their annual associational meeting because of the water, but they saw that their reports were there."[8]

Such commitment was impressive.

THIS I REMEMBER: Clearly Texas Baptists' ministry along the Rio Grande River would not have progressed in the fashion it did had it not been for the heart-response of Eula Mae Henderson and the mutual concerns of the presidents of Woman's Missionary Union of Texas. It seems Miss Henderson never forgot the deplorable conditions, the tremendous spiritual and physical needs, or the warm and wonderful people she met on her first River Ministry tour in February 1967. From that time on, she seems to have seen her role as doing all she could to create a climate in which the Holy Spirit could bring forth the responses God desired from His people.

Since Texas WMU has historically been on the cutting edge of missions, Miss Henderson and other Texas leadership immediately recognized that the corridor along the Rio Grande was indeed a unique mission field—and they took it personally. Through programming, films, trips, and allocations, River Ministry was featured in special events, Weeks of Prayer for State Missions, and the Mary Hill Davis Offerings. The first film, "This Is My Hand," a documentary; and the second film, "Rio Grande," premiered during these large conferences.

—Wilma Reed

Another 1967 event that was a special joy to Eula Mae was the 50th anniversary of Latin American work in Texas.

As described by Inez Hunt in *Century One: A Pilgrimage of Faith*, the meeting was held in San Antonio. Hortense (Mrs. I. A.) Palomo planned the session and presided since the elected president, Mrs. Paul Cuevas, had moved from the state. Mrs. Palomo was assisted by Noemí Cuevas, Texas WMU

Language Missions Director. During the meeting, Mrs. Palomo was elected President and Irene (Mrs. Carlos) Parades Vice-President. A history called *Sendas De Luz (Rays of Light)* was written through the efforts of a committee composed of Mrs. Rebecca Aguirre, Mrs. Adelina García, Mrs. G. G. Gonzáles, Mrs. Aurora I. Zarco, and Noemí Cuevas. The book was studied and featured throughout 1967.[9]

EMH rejoiced in the progress the group had made. Their first Lottie Moon and Annie Armstrong offerings, taken in 1931, totaled $150. In 1966, the year before the anniversary celebration, gifts had grown to $52,074.42 to the Cooperative Program, and $30,324.84 designated gifts.[10]

One of the areas of her work in which Eula Mae invested much time and energy on an ongoing basis involved the weeks of prayer. Each of the emphases was special, and each involved a specific area of mission work; she was committed to the totality. Like other state officers and staffers, her calendar was especially full during these times. The messages she brought in churches and associations reflected something of the core of her convictions—that people everywhere needed to hear the gospel. She believed it and she shared it with the Henderson touch—usually stories of mission work and missionaries she had visited. But promoting foreign and home missions came after themes, watchwords, hymns, and prayer guides were already selected and materials printed at the national level. The states had only to "pick it up and go from here," although that in itself was an ongoing and thought-provoking responsibility.

The Week of Prayer for State Missions, however, was appreciably more work-intensive. More than a year in advance, a committee must be selected and, with a series of prayerful meetings, a theme, watchword, hymns, and related items were chosen. Additionally, they must make suggestions on visual aids, prayer guides, and writers for the materials involved. It was a team effort that required much from many.

Involved in this process in 1969 was Lynn Yarbrough, then Art Director for the Baptist General Convention of Texas. "I was asked to design a poster promoting prayer and giving for state missions," Lynn recalled. "It was the first time I had been asked to do this, and I was told how important it was. I started by doing as much research as I could on allocations and needs so that I could communicate those needs in visual form."

Lynn described how she worked diligently to come up with an appropriate design. In this instance, she had two. Her practice was to present the material, explain what she deemed to be the objective, and then to interpret the design.

Arriving at Eula Mae's office after finishing her designs, she was warmly greeted, and in a few moments began her presentation to EMH and other workers.

"I watched her as I talked," Lynn said, "but I couldn't read her face. She listened intently, focusing on what I was saying but I couldn't tell whether she was pleased or displeased. She seemed to be neutral. I was concerned as I finished interpreting my first design because I had only two ideas to show.

"Anyway, having completed the first, I launched into the presentation of the second with even greater earnestness. I didn't know what I would do if both ideas were rejected. Again she listened closely and, again, I couldn't read her face. I felt downcast, thinking I had failed in this first important assignment for Woman's Missionary Union. I finished, and waited."

The room was silent; Eula Mae looked thoughtful. Neither Lynn nor any of the group present spoke. All of a sudden EMH's face lit up almost radiantly with a broad smile. She clapped her hands together and said, "Oh! We must have both posters!"

And it was done. One poster on one side of the paper, and the other on the reverse.

"After that," Lynn concluded, "I never feared for my presentations. I knew her procedure was to give me her full attention, to listen objectively, and then to make her decision.

Through the years, I continued to strive to communicate better the needs of the state missions offering."[11]

Eula Mae invited Lynn to interpret her design from the platform at the WMU House Party and later the Annual Meeting. This gave Lynn an introduction to public speaking. "I was petrified," she confessed, "yet I was honored she asked me. My admiration for her was such that I did a lot of stretching because I didn't want to disappoint her."

After several years, Lynn joined the staff of WMU, SBC where she served in several leadership positions, then was appointed a missionary to China in 1993. She recalled her days of mixing and mingling with Texas WMU as a time when "I learned a great deal about how to live a missions lifestyle."

Although the work in the Texas WMU office was heavy and demanding on many occasions, it had its lighter moments.

Some of these came with the opening of the mail. For several years Eula Mae kept a list of the "WMU Funnies."

"Last year you sent me several leaflets which I found very helpful," one woman wrote. Then she added, "Please send me everything I don't have." Then followed her name and address, but no listing of what she might have on hand.

"Please send prayer retread pamphlets for the coming year."

One request for help came to Texas WMU, but was apparently intended for Texas Baptist Men. "The Annie Armstrong Chapter has met four times. We would like to know if we could receive our Certificate of Registration and Annie Armstrong's address if possible as we would like to keep in contact with her." (The motive was appreciated.)

Another request, although valid, arrived via a somewhat different route. The message was "Please send any available helps and materials for promoting Lottie Moon Christmas Offering. Am setting up new WMU organization." The name and address of the church followed. What made it different? It was sent by ham radio from Texas to WMU, SBC in Birmingham. A ham radio operator there picked it up and relayed the request to WMU, SBC who, in turn, wrote to Texas WMU.

"WMU Funnies" came in more than written form through the years. Sometimes they happened on the platform. Eula Mae was noted for platform poise, but occasionally even she gave way to laughter when something unexpectedly humorous happened. Gerry Dunkin, who worked with EMH on associational and state levels, and later became President of Texas WMU, has told the story of an unforgettable associational meeting in which Eula Mae was the main speaker. Prior to her message, associational officers gave their respective reports. Community Missions had evolved into Mission Action, and what was termed "Literacy Missions" was on the upswing. The Mission Action Director, rounding out her report, included an emphasis on literacy. As she finished speaking, a lady seated near the front remarked to those around her, "She's right! Why, even on the way to this meeting, I saw litter on both sides of the highway. We simply must organize and clean it up!"[12]

Platform guests were convulsed. Even Eula Mae, who was next on the program, could not keep her composure.

She also enjoyed telling stories on herself—times when she got herself into awkward situations. One such tale was remembered by Linda (Mrs. Paul) Lyle, sometime soloist and conference leader for WMU events. After a dinner party, the group involved began to share humorous incidents. When Eula Mae's turn came, she regaled the group by relating the story of walking all the way up to the front of a church to speak at the traditional "Tuesday morning meeting time." As she did so, she noticed the puzzled look of the women present, and a funny feeling began to gnaw in her stomach. It turned out that she was in the wrong church, a Methodist church, in fact. The Baptist church was down the street, and both churches had women's groups meeting at the same time. The Methodist women graciously gave directions, and a red-faced Eula Mae hurried down the street, vowing to always check the name of the church if she had not been there before.[13]

Paul Lyle was involved in a humorous incident of another type. The Lyles and Eula Mae were both at a wedding reception. Seeing Eula Mae across the room, Mr. Lyle beckoned her over as if to tell her something. When she came, he mischievously pointed down and announced that he was now on the dance floor with Eula Mae Henderson. He loved it; so did she.

Glorieta, New Mexico was one of EMH's favorite places. She had enjoyed going there since the early 1950s when she attended "Pioneer Week." Her memories were vivid of those somewhat rustic days, and of eating "vanilla ice cream with peanut butter on top—that was our dessert." She also looked forward to the drive from Dallas to Glorieta, stopping at a steak house in west Texas which had "fabulous hot rolls," and watching the western landscape change from plains to canyons to the foothills of the mountains. Often on these journeys, she pointed out "cudja houses" to new staffers who made the trip with her for the first time.

Claudia Jones (Swain), who became GA/Mission Friends director in 1970, and Sheryl Churchill, who assumed state leadership of Acteens that same year, were with Eula Mae on one such trip. The trio was driving through the starkness of the windswept plains when Eula Mae pointed to a deserted, dilapidated house which stood alone on the landscape, and referred to it as a "cudja house."

Puzzled, Claudia took the bait and asked "A what?"

Delighted, Eula Mae explained, "That means 'cudja' (could you) love a man enough to live in a house like that?"

"Of course," Claudia reported, "neither Sheryl nor I had ever conceived of EMH thinking about topics such as that, and we laughed ourselves silly."[14]

Within the walls of the Baptist Building, her serious side prevailed, but her humor still bubbled up on occasion. Charles Lee Williamson, then Missions Director for the State Missions

Commission, recalled, "I can't be specific—I wish I could—but Eula Mae had a way of making a wry comment that would 'break up' the State Missions Commission Administrative Staff meetings."

WMU life decidedly had its humorous side through the years. Eula Mae knew the value of humor, to others, and to herself.

Meanwhile, the late 1960s saw the pace of WMU life continuing to increase. In 1968 Texas WMU held 25 regional meetings to introduce the women to impending changes in organization, names, and plan of work slated for 1970. Attendance at the meetings topped 9,000. Youth workers also had crowded calendars. Katharine Bryan as YWA Director planned and conducted five YWA House Parties with 4,696 registered. Additionally, since she also served as GA Director for two years, she did two GA Queens' Courts with 2,659 in attendance. Joyce Gill logged five regional Sunbeam Band leadership meetings reaching almost 600 workers.[15]

House Parties and Queens' Courts were some of Eula Mae's favorite meetings. Several times she was asked to lead the Call to Worship; many of these were later referred to as "classics."

Two that stand out in memory for some who were there were the series based on "Diamonds" done at a YWA House Party, and another entitled "Chosen" done at Queens' Court.

In the latter instance, Joy Pitts, longtime WMU worker with GAs and Acteens in Houston, and later a Promotional Vice-President, wrote, "The lights were dimmed and EMH was spotlighted sitting on a very tall stool, hands folded in her lap, her face tilted upward. My first thought was 'How does she sit up so straight?' Then I was caught up in her words. I can't recall everything she said, but we all sat spellbound. Each one of us felt that we were chosen by God, equipped by God, and empowered by God. Her own commitment was evident; that lent weight to her words."[16]

The times were memorable, but change was in the air foretelling days that would be different, but no less memorable.

Ophelia Humphrey had come to the end of a distinguished tenure as WMU President in 1968, and was succeeded by Inez Boyle (Mrs. H. C.) Hunt of Gregory, a locale she consistently referred to as "my village." Mrs. Hunt had been Recording Secretary, Mission Study Chairman, a Promotional Vice-President, and a popular conference leader. Petite in stature, she was large in every other way—in spirit, in vision, in commitment to missions.

Eula Mae, now in her third decade with Texas WMU, again felt "blessed indeed" in having another president well-versed in the work, highly literate, with an aura of warm friendliness that reached out and enveloped those around her. Additionally, like Mrs. Humphrey before her, Mrs. Hunt shared Eula Mae's ongoing interest in Hispanic work and had an easy familiarity with the Spanish language.

Anticipating the changes to come on the national level in 1970, young people's work, as well as workers, was being rearranged. Joyce Gill, who had headed Sunbeams since 1957, married William Kelsey in 1969, and resigned in 1970. Katharine Bryan moved from youth work to Baptist Young Women. The GA work was then combined with the new Mission Friends, and this was the position that Claudia Jones accepted.

The decade of the 70s was beckoning.

THIS I REMEMBER: Eula Mae was a very special person in my life. She modeled so many important traits, it is difficult to put into a few words what she meant to me and how she continues to influence me today.

In the years we worked together—sometimes in rather stressful situations—I never heard her say anything critical or unkind about anyone. If she couldn't find something good to say about another, she said nothing.

She was one who believed and practiced the principle that leaders should discover potential leaders, and provide them with encouragement and opportunities for growth. I am the grateful beneficiary of her commitment to that principle.

Eula Mae gave herself completely to the Lord and His calling. One of her favorite Scriptures was "He must increase, but I must decrease." (John 3:30) She modeled this; she lived by it.

She was also a delightful human being. I recall the survey trip along the Rio Grande as we prepared to launch the River Ministry. We knew the trip would not be easy, and I insisted we take tennis shoes and slacks. EMH did so, but never felt comfortable putting them on. However, at one point, we were preparing to wade the Rio Grande. She walked to the edge, sat down on the ground, put on tennis shoes, waded across, then promptly sat down again and donned her dress shoes.

She was an inspiration; she was delightful; she was unforgettable.
—Ophelia Humphrey

8

Changes, Choices... and Missions Firsthand

"If it doesn't change, it doesn't grow."

By the time the sweeping changes in Woman's Missionary Union structured by WMU, SBC were implemented in October 1970, state organizations had been in periods of intensive training for several months. Texas was no exception. To some local workers it seemed "We have to start all over again" because what was involved was so extensive: a new organizational structure, new implementation, new terminology, new magazines, and updated ways of doing missions within the various age-level groupings.

Eula Mae and Mrs. Hunt had been working toward the changeover date since the latter took office. The meetings had been many as the two women, along with other state leadership and staff, had dreamed, planned, and conducted training sessions on every level. In 1969, in the latter part of the training period, 28 workshops for local workers were held in Texas.

Mrs. Hunt, in her book *Century One: A Pilgrimage Of Faith*, described the time as "trying." Eula Mae's gray hair got grayer, but her brown eyes still sparkled. Both knew that the changes were necessary, reflecting the changing times and a changing world. On the national level, WMU had taken note of the sociological changes and moved to meet them. Uniform age grouping had been recommended for all Southern Baptist program organizations. WMU, SBC cooperated. Woman's Missionary Union would still be the umbrella term; it would include Baptist Women, Baptist Young Woman, Acteens, Girls in Action, and Mission Friends. Plans of work and terminology also changed. New magazines were introduced, although *Royal Service*, the flagship publication, remained.

Mrs. Hunt also remembered how she and Eula Mae were often asked, "Why did you change the organizations? We had already learned the work! Now we don't know who or where we are!"

And the reply was, "We had to learn it too, and it's hard! But let's remember that 'If it doesn't change, it doesn't grow.'[1] If the world changes and we don't, we lose out. Our purpose is unchanged—missions and missions education. We're just retooling to do a better job!"

Seemingly, it worked. On a national level, the WMU enrollment which had been dwindling since 1965, began to ebb more slowly, and then in the early years of the 1970s began an upward climb.[2]

Seemingly, also, the mission offerings were not adversely affected by the changes. Since missions giving was an integral part of the missions program, EMH collected stories along these lines and often shared them. One involved a woman from west Texas many years ago who decided, since she lived in a rural area, that she could "fatten up a pig and sell it for missions." However, in the heat of the summer, the pig died, and her fellow church members decided the woman would not be able to meet her pledge. However, she persevered, and came up with the idea of selling vegetables from her front porch. It worked. She had her missions money.

"And that kind of support we still have," Eula Mae stated as she told the story. "It may not involve either a pig or selling vegetables from your porch—it might be a sugar bowl on your kitchen table where you put in all your nickels and dimes every day. I knew one woman in Dallas who did that every year. And because of the dedication of women like that years ago, their children and grandchildren automatically come up to mission offering times today and think, 'What shall I give to Lottie Moon, or Annie Armstrong or Mary Hill Davis this year?' They do it because they remember a mother or grandmother who not only believed in it, but did something about it."[3]

To Eula Mae, true stories such as these not only fleshed out the importance of missions education and missions offerings, but also portrayed the "from one generation to the next" linkage essential to a successful missions program. She often referred to the missions offerings in her report to the Annual Meeting. On one occasion, she recognized every church that had posted an increase in the Mary Hill Davis Offering for State Missions in the past year. It was her feeling that those monies represented the "cutting edge" of missions.

But while 1970 had its special challenges, it also had its special joys. These were several.

The Baptist World Alliance met in Tokyo, and Mrs. Hunt, Eula Mae, and Mrs. Ralph Watson, a Promotional Vice-President, were among those attending. What made the occasion especially memorable for the Texas leadership was that Joy Phillips Fenner, by this time a missionary in Japan, was able to come to Tokyo from Fukuoka for a brief time of fellowship.

Meanwhile on the home front, Eula Mae and her staff planned a retirement reception for Nobie McGill who had filled several different slots in the WMU office; most recently she had been Mail Room Supervisor. She had been there "forever," she said. Actually, it was 17 years; she had long been "a part of the WMU family." Subsequently, Dorothy Chapman, wife of Robert Chapman who had been the last Royal Ambassador Secretary to serve under Texas WMU, filled that position.

FUN TIME—Inez Hunt (left) who led Texas WMU from 1968 until 1972 and was Eula Mae's sixth president, shares a light moment with musician Ken Medema, and Eula Mae at the Texas WMU House Party in the early 1970s. In the background is Taylor Pendley, then a BGCT staffer.

One of the summer highlights was in the form of a young musician named Ken Medema. Earlier, a student who was a summer missionary in New Jersey had encountered an unusual pianist and singer whose blindness had not deterred him from becoming both an outstanding musician and a witness for the Lord. The student recommended Ken Medema to Eula Mae for the upcoming House Party, and EMH, who tended to invite musicians she knew, felt led to extend an invitation to one she had never heard—an unusual procedure for her. Ken Medema came and he was one of the hits of the House Party. It was through this contact that he was introduced to Ron Owens, who in turn introduced him to Word Records. "And the rest is history," Eula Mae said. She felt privileged to have been a link in the chain.

The 1970 House Party also featured an autograph party. The honored guests were Ophelia Humphrey and Charles Lee Williamson, who co-authored *Sounds of the Seventies*, to be used with the Week of Prayer for State Missions material.[4] At that time, House Party programs offered more flexibility than Annual Meetings for showcasing something special which those in attendance went home talking about.

THIS I REMEMBER: I had many special times with Eula Mae, and she became my mentor. I appreciated her consistent commitment to "only the best," which showed in every phase of her work . I also remember that she liked to drink her coffee a scant one-half cup at a time; that way it would always be hot!
   —*Grace Dukes*

You couldn't travel with Eula Mae without knowing more about missions and missionaries—in fact, you couldn't be around her without absorbing missions! I also recall her "everyday faith;" her way of saying, "God is always more than adequate for every situation."
   —*Mary LaBauve*

Note: During Texas WMU House Party times at Baylor University, Grace and Mary served many years as hostesses in the dormitory where program personnel stayed.

The state youth leadership also chalked up advances. The GA Queens' Court at Baylor registered 2,638, and the first Acteens Celebration—a meeting for junior high girls—was held in Fort Worth. Celebration was the brainchild of Sheryl Churchill, who also inaugurated CIMTA (Christ In Missions Through Acteens), as well as the Texas Acteens Citation.[5]

"Eula Mae did not consider herself an authority on teenagers, but she brainstormed with me on these projects," Sheryl related. "She cared about teenagers, and cared that they had the best we could provide."

The Sounds of the Seventies, to borrow the Humphrey-Williamson phrase, seemed to indicate a rapid tempo as the decade began.

Eula Mae, who made it a habit to call attention to an individual or a group doing good work, seemed somewhat uncomfortable when the spotlight was turned on her. It happened when she received honorary doctorates in 1956 and 1970, and when the chapel at the Mexican Baptist Bible Institute in San Antonio was named in her honor in 1966. It also happened at other times when the women noticed that "She's been with us twenty years . . . or twenty five . . . or . . . " Such a time was 1971.

Minutes of the March 1971 Executive Board meeting recorded that "Mrs. Hunt asked Mrs. Earl Johnston, chairman, to bring a special report from the Finance Committee as follows: 'In recognition of Eula Mae Henderson's twenty-fifth anniversary . . . that the Executive Board authorize from the general fund $2,500 as a gift for a trip to a mission field of her choice.'"[6] She was also given an engraved silver bowl. She accepted the tributes graciously, then turned the focus of her comments to missions. The work beckoned.

The year 1972 rolled in with the familiar blend of the usual with the unusual. An interesting aspect of this was that when the "usual" got bigger, it was called "unusual." Then when this pattern kept repeating, the "unusual" became the "usual" again.

By whatever terminology, the early part of the year included four Acteen CIMTAs and 22 regional meetings. In the first instance, Eula Mae, in her monthly letter to board members, commented, "The echoes (from each meeting) have been good. Sheryl Churchill included specialized conferences for the Acteens and also a conference for leadership involving Mrs. Hunt, Marge Caldwell, and Sheryl."[7]

A little later, EMH wrote, "We have completed the 22 regional meetings! Those of us who made up the team of five for the various weeks felt the meetings were worthwhile. It was good to think again of the 'why' of our work with strong presentations on leadership, the total WMU family, and the tasks of WMU, all climaxed by Mrs. Woodson Armes' message on commitment."[8]

A major change for EMH early in the year involved the resignation of Dollie Culp, secretary and administrative assistant for Texas WMU, and the coming of Frances (Mrs. Dale) Stroope who had previously worked in the Baptist Building. In introducing Frances to the women, Eula Mae commented, "I think you would be interested in knowing that she is the mother of three sons, and all are 'preacher boys.'"[9]

THIS I REMEMBER: EMH was not only a wonderful supervisor and co-laborer, she was also my friend.

Before I came to the WMU office, she assured me that family was important to her, and she modeled it. She was interested in the families of those of us in the office. She encouraged me and prayed for me when my father was dying. She prayed for my children. She attended school plays with me to see our boys perform. She drove me to the hospital when I had surgery. She attended our sons' weddings. When our oldest son was appointed a missionary at Glorieta—which came during House Party—she asked Dollie Culp to take my place so I could be present for the appointment service. Later, she took a group to visit that same son in Sri Lanka. It made a world of difference to that young 25-year-old couple who felt like "It was a visit from home."

—Frances Stroope

As was her policy, EMH frequently shared highlights of WMU meetings around the state in her monthly letters to the board, as well as information she felt would be generally helpful. For instance, she wrote: "Mrs. T. E. Cooper of Waco Association (has sent us) publicity material pertaining to their Associational Missions Festival held February 17 at Columbus Avenue Baptist Church. They featured 32 booths with missionaries from five countries, and also spotlighted ministries conducted by the churches, areas of local needs, and community involvement programs.[10] Union Association (Mrs. A. J. Helmle) recently had a meeting featuring both home missions study conferences and mission action conferences. The combination of these two meets a real need—an idea worth remembering!"[11] Eula Mae also forwarded a request from missionaries in Nairobi, Kenya, who needed children's books, comic books, women's magazines, and reference books. The request came from Al and Peggy Cummins, who told about two libraries where people came to get books—people who were real prospects for the Lord's work. Experience had taught Eula Mae that board members were well able to both profit from shared ideas and respond to global needs.

On the national level, 1972 was the year of the first NAC (National Acteens Convention), held during WMU Week at Glorieta. Internationally, that same summer, Eula Mae and others were concerned about Marie Mathis, then serving a second term as WMU, SBC president. "Mrs. M" had left for Europe from the WMU, SBC Annual Meeting in Philadelphia; Eula Mae and Alma Hunt were among those to see her off from the hotel. Mrs. Mathis was headed for London and then to East Germany, where she would be for one week. At that time, neither the Baptist World Alliance nor the Foreign Mission Board had been able to get an American into East Germany. Alma Hunt had indicated that when Mrs. Mathis left Checkpoint Charlie, she would be out of touch with the world. She had only the names of six cities where she planned to visit Baptist churches.

Relating this, Eula Mae added, "Let us have a part in her ministry there as we pray for her."[12]

This was done. Happily, "Mrs. M" returned safely.

Between the years 1972 and 1982, Eula Mae conducted six mission tours. Three were to Europe, one to New England, one to the Orient, and one to Africa. The trips were usually from two to three weeks in length, with the size of the tour groups ranging from 16 to 30. In each instance, EMH planned a special highlight which frequently was a surprise to participants. Evelyn and Bill Beaird of Garland and Eula Mae's sister, Erma Barnett, accompanied her on all the trips; Dorothy and George Goff participated in all but one; several other persons "became addicted," as they phrased it, and went as schedules and finances permitted.

Evelyn Beaird recalled incidents from that initial trip in 1972. "We had a three-day retreat at Chateau d'Oex in Switzerland to climax our trip," she said. "Our special treat was to meet theologian Francis Schaeffer—knickers, high socks, and all! EMH had asked him to speak to us, and he did. Most of us were completely awe-struck.

"Another incident that I recall had no relationship to Dr. Schaeffer, but I do remember that it was in Switzerland where we had our first meeting in a bar. Actually, we met in a number of places during our journeys, depending on what was available. In this instance, a bar was what was available, and I have a clear mental picture of EMH sitting on a bar stool and leading us in singing 'Happy Birthday' to someone in the group. We loved it!"[13]

In those 1970s trips, one highlight was a trip to the Taj Mahal, although this had not been kept a secret. Another was attending a performance of the Passion Play in Oberammergau, Germany. Still another was to visit the home of Corrie ten Boom in Haarlem, the Netherlands.

Eula Mae's tours were, in every sense, travel with a purpose. As she looked back on them, she made the comment, "In all of these tours where I have taken a group, I have sought to contact the missionaries, and have that kind of experience for the people in the tour group. It wasn't just sight-seeing, but a learning experience with missionaries at different mission points. In other words, it's seeing missions firsthand."

Inez Hunt finished her eventful tenure as President in the fall of 1972. At a luncheon honoring her, Eula Mae quoted Horace Mann and said, "'A house without books is like a room without windows.' To know Inez Hunt and her love of books is to know that her house has many windows, for she has many books. And through her windows, she has looked out on a very wide horizon." EMH went on to describe Mrs. Hunt's many-faceted contribution to the work of WMU and then added, "I respect her; her judgment, her sense of loyalty, her recognition of God's demand upon people, and her own appreciation of all people. I value the sharing times we have had. She has been easy to love and I have felt her love in a very real way for our mutual work, and for me."[14]

In her final message as President, Mrs. Hunt structured her address along the lines of "Giant Step," an enlistment plan introduced by WMU, SBC. She mentioned the "giant steps" being taken as the Texas WMU House Party continued to grow, affording opportunities of enlarged training. She referred to the Latin American work, the River Ministry, and the growth in Baptist Young Women membership. She also mentioned the state meeting for the wives of pastors and church staffers, saying "It was a first, but we hope not the last." In conclusion, she encouraged her listeners to continue their "giant steps" toward spiritual development, and quoted Mary Hill Davis, "God does not consider our prospects. He honors our faith."

The new President stepping to the fore was Mauriece (Mrs. Earl) Johnston who had just finished her term as Recording Secretary, and, at different times, had been President of San Antonio Association, district five, and district six. Mrs. Johnston's first involvement with WMU had been as a GA in Calvary Baptist Church, Waco; that early interest was sustained by different positions in various places through the years. Like other state presidents before and after her, she had been active in Hispanic work. Also, she had taught intermittently at the Mexican Baptist Bible Institute in San Antonio. Perhaps in part because of this connection, Teresa (Mrs. Pete) Luna was asked to give the dedication prayer in Abilene at the time Mrs. Johnston was elected. Mrs. Luna prayed in Spanish, and Eula Mae felt like this was "just right!"

Mrs. Johnston's first experience on the Texas WMU Executive Board had begun several years earlier in 1960. Having been elected a member-at-large from district five, she

COMPARING NOTES—Eula Mae and her seventh president, Mauriece Johnston (right) chat with Dr. Sidlow Baxter at a Texas WMU House Party in the mid-1970s. Dr. Baxter was one of Eula Mae's favorite authors, and one whom she quoted. Mrs. Johnston led Texas WMU from 1972 to 1976, and again from 1980 to 1984 after Eula Mae's retirement.

had traveled to Dallas by car with Inez Hunt, Cleo (Mrs. Ernest) Pierce and Barbara (Mrs. Grady) West. "I remember that trip—that long trip!" she said later. "It was in the days of hats and petticoats, so you can imagine what the car was like. We spent one night on the road, and then in Dallas stayed at a downtown hotel. The board sessions were at First Baptist Church."

Mrs. Johnston went on to describe how she had felt when she first walked in and just stood there, not knowing quite what to do. Eula Mae saw this new board member looking hesitant, not talking much. Right away EMH came over and said, "Mrs. Johnston, I want you to meet another new board member, Mona Townes, from Muleshoe."

The two women then began talking and Mrs. Johnston felt enveloped in friendliness. It was a good beginning.

THIS I REMEMBER: I have always said that Eula Mae made each president with whom she worked look good. And she did! Her daily telephone contact with me was a powerful impact on my life in the area of friendship as well as spiritual development. In the former instance, she was genuinely interested in my family as well as our ministry, and included us in her prayers. Spiritually, her focus was on "We are laborers together with God," and I remember her emphasis on "I am only one woman, but I am one woman . . . I can pray, I can give, I can go."

A very practical bit of advice she gave me was in the realm of readiness. She would say, "Mauriece, if you have to speak on a moment's notice, always have favorite Scriptures and poems or quotations ready." A good idea!

I am also grateful to Eula Mae for making a way for me to meet great Christians of our day. She would schedule breakfast, lunch, a ride in a taxi to the airport—whatever plan she could come up with—to get to know great Christians such as Corrie ten Boom.

All in all, even today I can feel her influence on my life as though I had just talked with her. What a blessing!
—Mauriece Johnston.

Mrs. Johnston's first tenure as President (she later served again from 1980 to 1984) was, for all practical purposes, "jump started." At the conclusion of the Annual Meeting at which she was elected, she and Eula Mae were approached by Frank Burress, then working with the three associations that comprised Southern Baptist work in Minnesota-Wisconsin. He thanked the women for all that Texas WMU had done in helping train the women of his area, and stated that he thought it was now time for Minnesota-Wisconsin to have its own WMU House Party. He concluded by asking, "Will you put that in motion?"

Of course they would. It could not happen in 1973 because of budget restraints and the need to locate a proper site for the meeting. But it could in 1974. The Texas leadership called together the three women who headed the associations (Minnesota-Wisconsin did not have a state Director at that time) and, together with Mrs. Johnson and Eula Mae, plans were set in motion for their first WMU Conference. It happened as planned in the summer of 1974. Texas sent 23 trained women to the event held on the campus of Northwestern College at Roseville, Minnesota. Included in that number were Mrs. Johnston and Eula Mae, as well as the missionary speaker, Joy Phillips Fenner, then on furlough from Japan.[15]

Plans for the Minnesota-Wisconsin event, and the carrying out of those plans, made up one memorable page in the Texas WMU book of activities—and certainly an important page.

THIS I REMEMBER: I am one of those who Eula Mae Henderson "turned on" to missions in Minnesota-Wisconsin—and I'm so glad she did!

It all started many years ago. I was a Christian, active in my church, yet missions was somewhere on the periphery of my life. Then I went to a WMU meeting in Milwaukee where Eula Mae was the speaker. When she started, she caught my interest. Before she finished, I was totally enthralled with what she said, the way she said it, and who she was. I had never heard it that way before. Right then and there, I decided that what she talked about—a missions lifestyle, missions education—was to be a big part of my life.

And it has been. God has been very good to open doors, and give me opportunities of service. I am grateful to Him and to Eula Mae.

—Ann McDonald, former President, Minnesota-Wisconsin WMU

Also on tap in the early 1970s was one occasion that always rang the bell for Eula Mae—the wedding of one of her staffers. Claudia Jones was married to Richard Swain of Dallas in April of 1973.

"Eula Mae enjoyed my wedding preparations as much as I did," commented Claudia later. "She loved all my nieces and nephews who came to visit the office. Once, she even sent Sheryl Churchill out to buy a tea set to entertain Elizabeth and Elliott DeLoach, two preschoolers coming to see their aunt in her office. And of course we took pictures of them having a tea party with Eula Mae Henderson!"[16]

Such pictures made for an interesting scrapbook. They also tell another side of life at WMU.

Other ongoing activities claiming time and attention along professional lines included the Big Sister concept in associational work, whereby a strong association lent support and assistance to a less developed one. This dovetailed with Eula Mae's idea of reaching out and sharing with each other, which she promoted on both the local and associational levels.

The year 1973 also marked changes at the Baptist General Convention of Texas when James Landes was elected Executive Secretary of the BGCT since T. A. Patterson was retiring. Eula Mae was very appreciative of Dr. Patterson's ongoing commitment to missions as exemplified by the Japan New Life Crusade and the beginning of the River Ministry. Dr. Patterson's wife, Roberta Turner Patterson (affectionately called "Honey"), had held a number of WMU positions including Recording Secretary and Historian, in addition to authoring *Candle By Night*, the Diamond Jubilee history of Texas WMU published in 1955.

At the Annual Meeting that year, Texas WMU honored Dr. and Mrs. Patterson with a luncheon, and welcomed Dr. and Mrs. Landes.

Through the years, Eula Mae sought to highlight and strengthen the relationship between Texas WMU and the pastors of the state. Mrs. Johnston, a pastor's wife, was equally strong in this area. As a special feature of the 1974 Annual Meeting, four pastors were featured, one at each session, telling what WMU meant to his church.

Inez Hunt, in the book *Century One: A Pilgrimage Of Faith* described the sessions: "Glen Godsey, pastor of Primera Iglesia Bautista, Plainview, cited numerous ways WMU had led the church to meet physical and spiritual needs in his community. Harold Branch, pastor of St. John's Baptist Church, Corpus

Christi, and Second Vice-President of the Baptist General Convention of Texas, closed his remarks with the statement, 'If God should move the WMU out of our church, I would have only one sermon to preach: Farewell, gentlemen!' Leroy Kemp, pastor of First Baptist Church, Belton, evaluated WMU on two questions: 'What if there were no WMU?' and 'What would be the development of our denomination in Christian missions if there were no WMU?' Darrell Robinson, pastor of First Baptist Church, Pasadena, spoke of the mission action ministry of the WMU in his church and his gratitude for being a pastor of a strong WMU."[17]

The firsthand evaluations by the pastors were well received.

Before the year was out, Eula Mae and the entire Texas leadership team rejoiced in the fact that a total of 28 Latin American scholarships had been granted—the largest at any one time—and that Valley Baptist Academy graduated its largest class, 23. EMH was the speaker, the first woman so honored.

A staff change was also a part of the picture in the mid-seventies, with Katharine Bryan taking on the duties of Baptist Women Director, in addition to her Baptist Young Women responsibilities. As a group, the officers and staff were feeling the need to think in terms of "hundreds." America's bicentennial celebration was coming up in 1976, and the centennial year for Texas WMU would be celebrated in 1980.

The bicentennial influence dominated many of the WMU meetings during that year, with "red, white, and blue everywhere," as Eula Mae described it. WMUers across the age levels, from Mission Friends through Baptist Women, responded.

Looking toward the Texas centennial, Mrs. Johnston appointed Jean (Mrs. Leroy) Kemp as Centennial Chairman, and plans were initiated for the upcoming celebration. Texas was divided into six regions, and a centennial leader appointed for each.

The year 1976 also brought another change. Mrs. Johnston had come to the end of her tenure; she was succeeded by Huis Coy (later Egge). The new president, like her predecessors, had a strong WMU background, having served as Promotional Vice-President; chaired the Week of Prayer for State Missions Committee when the River Ministry was initiated; and since she had studied law, twice chaired the Bylaws Committee.

The Annual Meeting in which Mrs. Coy was elected had a surprise feature that was not on Eula Mae's copy of the program. She was given a heart-shaped diamond necklace to commemorate her 30 years with Texas WMU.

She wore it with gratitude and with pride.

9

Shadows, Sunshine . . . Remembrances, Retirement

"I am debtor to the Greeks . . . and to many others!"

"A problem is really an opportunity in disguise," but Eula Mae must have felt in 1977 that her opportunities were weighing a bit heavily on her. Even her characteristic optimism may have been challenged when difficulties arose in her personal life, her family life, and even her professional life. Her gray hair was now almost white, and her brown eyes reflected the introspection the days demanded.

In January of that year, in writing to the Texas WMU Executive Board, she had shared news of staff and volunteer activity from different associations, as well as promotional ideas that had crossed her desk. Then, toward the close of her letter, she added that she had just learned from her doctor that she must have immediate surgery for a breast tumor. Briefly, she outlined the plans of "who would do what" in the office during her absence. Then, in typical EMH fashion, she turned the focus away from herself and commented on the new Texas WMU centennial stationery: "How do you like it? Isn't it beautiful? It will be a constant reminder of our anniversary in 1980, and that is exciting!"

Her sister, Erma Barnett, came to Dallas for EMH's surgery, as did several close friends. The operation went well, although the tumor proved to be malignant and treatment was recommended as a precautionary measure. Eula Mae was out of the office for four weeks, spending several days in Oklahoma City. She and her sister were both careful not to mention the illness to her mother whose own health was precarious. To Mrs. Henderson, it just seemed that Mae (her name for her older child) had come for a visit.

Cards and flowers arrived in abundance. Upon her return to the office, Eula Mae thanked the women for their support and thoughtfulness, commenting on the good care she had received. "I am debtor to the Greeks . . . and many others," she wrote, expressing appreciation to the medical staff who had attended her and friends who had supported her with flowers, cards, visits, and most of all, prayer. She added a humorous note: "Upon observing all the company and attention I had in the hospital, a friend said she wants to register as a WMU personality if she ever checks into Baylor!"

She concluded by saying simply, "I have read the Bible with a new perspective, and there has been some adjusting of priorities. I continue to be grateful for the reality of God, and for the little motto which has hung in my office for several years: 'The Lord is always more than adequate for every situation.'"[1]

March brought another problem in that radiation treatments were scheduled the same days as the Executive Board sessions. She solved the dilemma by slipping off and going to the hospital on her lunch hour. It was important to her not to miss any of the board meeting. In addition to committee work, reports, business, inspiration, and fellowship, there were the centennial plans to be discussed, not to mention the presence of out-of-state guests such as Marie Mathis and Catherine Allen from WMU, SBC. "I really need to be there," she said. And she was.

With summer came another hard time. Her mother passed away in July. Mrs. Henderson had been in ill health for several months, and lived in Lackey Manor on the outskirts of Oklahoma City. When the situation became critical, Eula Mae went to Oklahoma City and she and Erma sat with their mother for the last days of her life.

The Hendersons were an unusually close family; the daughters felt their loss keenly. Friends traveled to Oklahoma City to be with Eula Mae and Erma during these days, and EMH subsequently returned to Dallas. Later, she confided to Huis Coy Egge, "I miss my mother so much during the difficult times because I could always count on the fact that she prayed for me every day."

In late summer, Eula Mae's time was more than taken up with not only House Party, but with several other special events, as well. The House Party itself featured the premiere performance of "Harvest," the musical commissioned by Texas WMU which would later be a part of the Week of Prayer for State Missions. With music written by Dick Anthony and lyrics by Bill O'Brien, the event opened the House Party on Tuesday night. The musical was also featured at Ridgecrest and Glorieta, in varied Texas churches and associations, and was later presented overseas in Jerusalem.

The evening following "Harvest" at the House Party highlighted the 10th anniversary of the River Ministry.

Two meetings pertaining to language missions were also much in her thoughts these months. One was the WMU Latin American meeting held in early summer each year, this time in Galveston. Eula Mae wrote to board members, "Our Mary Godsey will preside, and I am anticipating hearing Mrs. Coy as she speaks in Spanish!" After the meeting she referred to the prayertime led by Irene (Mrs. Carlos) Parades and the afternoon reception which honored the past presidents of Texas WMU Latin American work.

THIS I REMEMBER: *Eula Mae's leadership qualities, in my opinion, were unsurpassed. She was a strong, yet gentle leader, always giving co-workers the privilege of participating in decision-making. Her creativity was remarkable; she never ran out of new ideas.*

One of the greatest things she did for missions and missions education was to develop and train leaders, equipping women to serve not only in Texas WMU, but in the SBC as well.

She believed in Texas women, and she was willing to share leadership with others.

To me, it seemed that her personality drew people to her. They followed her as they saw her following Jesus. I have often said that she was the greatest Christian I knew. I wanted to emulate her.

—Huis Coy Egge

Another emphasis during these months was the Associational Language Missions Seminar held in September in Dallas, with Doris Díaz of WMU, SBC as the leader, assisted by Rosa Martínez from Nashville. Texas leadership included Mary Godsey, Viola Mendiola, Isabel Estrada, María Merino, and Marcella Cásarez. EMH felt the growing need for giving emphasis to the work among Hispanics, as this group represented an ever-growing segment of the Texas population. Her thinking was "WMU is for all Texas Baptist women and children." She respected Hispanic heritage by promoting meetings and workshops conducted in Spanish, and also encouraged Latin American women to participate in the ongoing work of Texas WMU.

EMH seldom allowed her personal problems to surface in her professional life. However, 1977 was difficult in both areas. On the personal side was her surgery, the radiation which followed, and the death of her mother. On the professional side, she encountered more staff movement than she had ever experienced. Sheryl Churchill had already resigned in late 1976 to accept the position of Baptist Young Women Consultant with WMU, SBC. Katharine Bryan resigned in 1977 to pursue a doctorate at Southwestern Baptist Theological Seminary. Claudia Jones Swain left her GA/Mission Friends position that same year to seek a graduate degree and return to teaching. Each had served Texas WMU well; each had made a decided contribution. But now, in the pattern of many who worked as directors of age-level organizations, they had moved on.

Barbara Curnutt came in March of 1977 to fill the Acteens Director's slot. That left two open positions, so Eula Mae, Barbara, state officers, and other volunteers filled in as needed.

In 1978, Nell Carter, who had been an editorial assistant at WMU, SBC, came as GA/Mission Friends Director and Dorothy Miller, who had been on the staff of First Baptist Church in Dallas, arrived to assume Baptist Women/Baptist Young Women responsibilities.

The year had begun well in January with reference to a project of personal interest to Eula Mae. At some earlier time, the Texas WMU board had decided to put out a WMU Executive Board Recipe Book with recipes from any board member wishing to submit one or more. In January, EMH wrote to remind the women to submit recipes by February 1 since the books were to be distributed at the March board meeting. "I think we would all welcome unusual recipes," she wrote. "You may even have a recipe for a sauce, a gravy, or biscuits. Just be sure to include your name and address." They did. The recipe book was a sound success.

Eula Mae herself was an enthusiastic collector of recipes and someone who enjoyed cooking and entertaining. By this time in her career, she had adopted the plan of sending to board members each December a Christmas recipe. Over the years, the yuletide recipes made quite a collection.

Another winter highlight was the WMU, SBC Executive Board meeting which included promotional sessions, and this year a special dedication of a new addition to the national office. The annual meeting for national leadership and state staffers, along with state presidents, had long been a part of Eula Mae's life. This year she felt like it had been outstanding, and described it in writing: "Executive sessions, general sessions, age-level times, committee meetings, group sessions, presentations, special luncheons, and seminars! One of the most interesting times took place on Wednesday afternoon with the dedication of the WMU building addition, followed by an open house. WMU had purchased the building in 1951, added two floors, and this year, a triangular addition which added 5,000 square feet to the facility. Catherine Allen supervised the decorating which was typical of WMU and missions, and beautifully done. When Mrs. Coy and I asked her about her decorating experience, she laughed and said, 'I helped Mrs. Mathis hang pictures one time!'"[2]

Bold Mission Thrust, the SBC plan to reach all peoples with the gospel by the year 2000, was an ongoing theme in Texas in 1978. All-out participation was encouraged. A special session for women was a part of the Evangelism Conference, with Peggy Cummins and Barbara Cunningham in charge. Also, "Women in the Church," a new course in the College-Level Curriculum Series (Sunday School Board) was written by Minette (Mrs. Huber) Drumwright who had served as a Promotional Vice-President of Texas WMU.

The excitement permeated the WMU Executive Board meeting in March, and Eula Mae, along with others, used it as the centerpiece of her report to the board. "Missions is always a somebody . . . a someplace . . . and a somebody else," she said. "You and I are a part of the continuing story of missions, and a part of that story hasn't been written yet." She then proceeded to share quotations from each of the 12 presidents of Texas WMU who had served between 1880 and the late 1970s, showing how each had written a chapter in the continuing story of missions. She concluded with Huis Coy (Egge), then president, who had inspired the women by saying, "Through the years, Woman's Missionary Union has had great leaders; and now, it is you and me. God is depending on us in this generation!"[3]

Added emphasis to Bold Mission Thrust was also a part of the meeting when James Landes, Executive Secretary of the Baptist General Convention of Texas, and Richard Faling, consultant in the Mission Support Department, both addressed the board. The former spoke on "Texas and Bold Mission" and the latter on "Church Achievement . . . Bold Mission."

And it was happening. Eula Mae had been impressed by the hum of accelerated missions activity. A family from Dallas had gone to Florida to help with a migrant Vacation Bible School. Three Texas WMU Board members had volunteered to go at their own expense to Utah-Idaho to lead conferences on missions education. Workers from Texas were also going to Minnesota-Wisconsin to help the women there stage their own House Party, while another eight women were headed for Billings, Montana, to help those in the Northern Plains area. Bob and Jean Dixon of Dallas had already gone to St. Cloud, Minnesota, to begin a church, and had come home to start a Bible study in their own neighborhood. Mr. And Mrs. Raymond Matthews of San Marcos signed up to serve with the

Christian Service Corps in Carlin, Nevada. Dorothy and L. M. Commander of Robertson Association went to Iowa as volunteers for several months. Workers from Union Association were making preparations to journey to Portland, Oregon, to help with new work at 25 potential church start sites.

It was also happening on the associational level. Avenues for service were being showcased. For example, Nelda Kearns (Gerbine) of Tarrant Association reported on an associational mission action fair which featured several types of volunteer service, including a Seaman's Center. When opportunities were presented, the women responded.

In May, the Baptist General Convention of Texas staged a three-day event in Dallas called "Bold Mission Planning for Associational Advance." Attendance was excellent. The conference for associational WMU directors attracted some 88 participants, and featured not only Texas leadership, but also Carolyn Weatherford (Crumpler), Executive Director of WMU, SBC.

At this point Bold Mission Thrust seemed to be well on its way, and Eula Mae was caught up in its spirit. This unprecedented missions emphasis, plus the upcoming centennial year of Texas WMU, made for eventful days.

In the late spring of 1978, Eula Mae used her three-week vacation to direct a tour to the Orient. It proved to be one of her best. Upon her return, she wrote "The sojourners to the Orient are back! My three-week vacation was one like I have never had before!" She spoke of being in Japan with Joy and Charlie Fenner, and the privilege of staying in a Japanese home. She spoke glowingly of the work of the Bill Wallace Memorial Hospital in Pusan, Korea, and the hospital in Bangalore, India, where Dr. Rebekah Naylor served. She mentioned the heat, the Taj Mahal, and the seminary in Taiwan. She told of the group's being entertained by Kaaren Hitt, daughter of Vera Hammock, Corpus Christi Associational WMU Director.

"In Hong Kong," she wrote, "we had 17 missionaries as our guests for a buffet lunch. In Sri Lanka, our 24 hours were full ones; we have four missionaries there—Bob and Joy Cullen, and Mike and Kay Stroope. We were their first Southern Baptist visitors. In each place, we wanted to stay longer."

"There is much more to tell, but there will be other opportunities." Then she added a sentence which illustrated her stewardship of missions money, "While we were away, postage went up, so we will seek to make every letter from our office really count."[4]

The 25th Anniversary WMU House Party in August 1978 aroused interest a number of months in advance. Plans had been announced to bring to the event many individuals who had taken part in that first House Party. "Promises To Keep" had been the theme and it was repeated for the anniversary. Eula Mae was delighted with the printed program. She told the women, "Plans for the anniversary printed program are exciting. It will really be a souvenir program to keep. Lynn Yarbrough (then Art Director for BGCT) is doing it again!"

Many in the Baptist Building, as well as around the state, let it be known that the event would be special. At one point Charles McLaughlin, Director of the BGCT State Missions Commission, sent a note to Eula Mae to say "This Twenty-Fifth Anniversary House Party will undoubtedly be blessed of God, and I look forward to being there. I'm praying for you every day."

Program participants who led at the first House Party and planned to be at the 1978 event included Juliette Mather, long-time WMU, SBC staffer who had also served overseas with the Foreign Mission Board; Alma Hunt who had now retired from

WMU, SBC and was living in Roanoke, Virginia; Mary Etheridge and Nina Gillespie who had been home missionaries in Arizona; Mrs. Harry Wigger, missionary to Thailand; Edna Frances Dawkins, Richmond, Virginia; Helen Fling, Birmingham, Alabama; Sybil Leonard Armes, Texas, and others.

By June, twice the number of WMUers had pre-registered for the House Party as had the year before. By early July, dormitory space on the Baylor campus was gone and the state office was sending out reservation cards for those who could make their own lodging arrangements. "We will stop," Eula Mae indicated, "when registration reaches the maximum that Waco Hall can hold."

The early response laid to rest a concern that some had expressed earlier. Each summer, WMU Week at Glorieta and the Texas WMU House Party were major summer training events. Some felt that each would hurt the other in attendance. Not so in 1978. At Glorieta, which featured a combined WMU and Brotherhood Week, attendance was between 400 and 500 over the previous year, as Eula Mae observed. And obviously the House Party was attracting record numbers. Martha (Mrs. O. L.) Walker, WMU Director of Gulf Coast Association, who had taken 29 women to Glorieta and had reservations for 45 to the House Party, put the matter in perspective when she wrote, "With all this training, we ought to be *bold* in every way!"[5]

The House Party lived up to expectations—and then some—with the general sessions featuring historical highlights. Among the wide variety of conference offerings was a significant new entry, the first conference for women from Black Baptist churches. It was led by Bennie Hancock of Wichita Falls, the first Black Associational WMU Director in Texas.[6]

August also brought wedding bells to the state office from two directions: Huis Coy married Elvis Egge, and Nell Carter became the bride of Jim Branum.

The Annual Meeting, which followed in the fall in Austin, was a good one with more than a thousand in attendance. A highlight was the presentation by the centennial coordinators of "Once Upon a Time . . . in Austin." This was later printed in *The Helper* so that churches and associations might use it.

The last two months of the year closed on an optimistic note. At Thanksgiving, EMH, with a sense of gratitude and a consciousness of blessings large and small, wrote, "Those of us at 102 Baptist Building are grateful for Mrs. Egge and our other state officers, members of our Executive Board and (all) who join us in being 'Laborers together with God.' I hope this Thanksgiving time will include for you a time of gratitude for every small thing we so often take for granted. How good it is to be able to distinguish between warmth and cold, and to see a small leaf flying in the wind."[7]

When Eula Mae looked at the 1979 schedule, she took a deep breath: WMU, SBC would be having its Annual Meeting in her state, in Houston. Texas activities included six Mini-House Parties to prepare for the centennial, ten area clinics for associational workers, day and evening associational workshops for local leaders, as well as associational mission support institutes, a seminar for Baptist Young Women directors, four Celebrations for Acteens, language missions events, three weeks of prayer—not to mention board meetings, the House Party, WMU Conference at Glorieta, and the Texas WMU Annual Meeting with a GA Rally preceding it which would attract 500 girls. Nell Carter Branum announced in April that she would be leaving in May after one year of service as GA/Missions Friends Director; Eula Mae wrote, "We can be grateful that we had her this long." Marsha Spradlin was elected at the August board meeting to replace her. Meanwhile, local churches and associations were promoting the centennial goals, together with the ongoing emphasis on Bold Mission Thrust.

By the latter years of her tenure, EMH was writing an average of two letters a month to board members, which sometimes gave her and Texas WMU the opportunity to be of assistance in an unusual way. In April of 1979, a tornado struck the Wichita Falls-Vernon area. Eula Mae and Mrs. Egge, immediately concerned, decided that perhaps churches and associations could be of help, not only with prayers, but also with specific household items and church furnishings and equipment. After finally being able to reach Mrs. Bennie Hancock, Associational WMU Director in Wichita Falls, EMH discovered some specific needs and sent to the board names and addresses of churches destroyed or damaged, as well as the names and addresses of pastors whose homes were destroyed or damaged. In urging the women to help, she wrote, "Imagine how great it would be (for those in need) to hear from people all over the state who offer, along with their prayer support, a willingness to be of some specific help. Some pastors or church staff may be in need of books if their libraries were lost; some may need household goods such as sheets and towels; some would welcome a check to buy some of these things."[8]

As usual, the women responded.

As time approached for WMU Conference at Glorieta, stories abounded about the Fourth of July events that would be a part of the program, since Independence Day came during that time. Included were rumors about a special Independence Day parade. When that day arrived, there were Barbara Curnutt, Carolyn Weatherford (Crumpler), and June Whitlow waving from horseback, along with others. Eula Mae, who had been known to ride a donkey on River Ministry tours during her earlier years, was not anxious to participate in this equestrian event. There was a parade—with the color guard and flags—and each state had a float. "The state Brotherhood did ours," Eula Mae explained. Then, in front of New Mexico Hall, there was a special musical program with patriotic songs, state songs, and fun songs.

For the House Party that summer, EMH and Mrs. Egge decided to invite pastors from different parts of the state to come to the event as the guests of Texas WMU. Pastors had been invited previously as program participants; this time they were simply the guests of Texas WMU. Then, as usual, letters of appreciation came to the WMU office, but this time some of them were different. "I must confess," Eula Mae said, "that many of the most interesting letters have come from the pastors who were there. I wish we had started the plan 26 years ago!" This "happenstance," along with the parade of Baptist Young Women which took place on Wednesday morning under Dorothy Miller's leadership, was among the highlights that Eula Mae loved to recall.

Appropriately enough, the Annual Meeting held that year in Lubbock continued the strong Bold Missions Thrust emphasis, blended with splashes of centennial flavor, since the 100th year observance for Texas WMU was about to begin. On Tuesday morning, the meeting featured the 12 presidents of Woman's Missionary Union of Texas for the 100 years. Living presidents—Mrs. Black, Mrs. Humphrey, Mrs. Hunt, Mrs. Johnston, and Mrs. Egge—played themselves. Each woman spoke as if she were simply remembering, and each president was dressed appropriately for the period in which she served. The occasion brought back many memories to Eula Mae. "I have worked with eight of the twelve presidents," she later commented. "And I knew another, Mrs. B.A. Copass, who was president when I was in Southwestern Seminary. Certainly you would know that these women have blessed my life immeasurably."

Looking backward . . . looking ahead . . . Mrs. Egge expressed how both she and Eula Mae felt at the time of the 1979 meeting, "My head sometimes doesn't know if it is going forward or backward as I serve as the link between the 100 years behind us and the new century which calls to us. But I have been so excited about Bold Mission Thrust that I am doing a lot of my living in the Now and Future!"

The year 1980 saw both the climax of the Texas WMU centennial celebration, and Eula Mae's retirement after 34 years. The year also marked the end of her lengthy service in one of the Junior departments of First Baptist Church in Dallas. Millie Kohn, longtime Junior Director at First Baptist, wrote of EMH, "For thirty years she was the strongest influence for real missions in our division for fourth-, fifth-, and sixth-graders. Her impact left an indelible impression, on not only the children, but also the adults with whom she worked. We followed her because she personified what she represented; she led by example."[9]

THIS I REMEMBER: Week by week, as Eula Mae visited mission areas, she would bring back stories of these places and people to her 11-year-olds (in Sunday School) at First Baptist, Dallas. It may have been a story about the little Indian boy on the reservation, or the child who drank clean water from the well our children had helped raise money for. She gave meaning to missions. Her influence is being lived out in the lives of scores of men and women serving all over the world who went to First Baptist (during her 30 years there). For someone of Eula Mae's influence and stature to teach children, is indicative of her whole life. To claim her as mentor and friend is one of the sweetest blessings of my life.
—Millie Kohn

FOR YESTERDAY AND FOR TOMORROW—*Huis Coy Egge, the eighth and final president with whom Eula Mae served, joins EMH in leading the "Centennial Walk" in October, 1980, commemorating the past, and looking forward to the future. Women from across the state journeyed to Austin to celebrate the 100th birthday of Texas WMU. A part of that occasion was the walk from the current First Baptist Church in Austin to the site of the former edifice where Texas WMU was organized in 1880. Mrs. Egge headed Texas WMU from 1976 to 1980.*

On the WMU calendar, the usual activities crammed the calendar that year, but so did the unusual. The long-planned Mini-House Parties planned for the centennial unreeled on schedule. Centennial cups were available, not to mention thimbles. The March board meeting also had centennial place cards made especially for the session by Mighty River Handcrafts, featuring not only the centennial but also Eula Mae's name. She was also given an elaborate book with notes and pictures from board members, plus an IBM Selectric typewriter, and a desk pen set from Minnesota-Wisconsin WMU.

The GA Super Saturday Spectaculars, under Marsha Spradlin's direction, attracted approximately 2,000 girls, the first being in Fort Worth and the second in San Antonio. Barbara Curnutt promoted a Missions Opportunities Weekend for Acteens; this was followed in early summer by a mission trip to Brazil taken by 12 Acteens from Windsor Park Baptist Church in Austin with their leader, Jan Sutton. Soon it was time for the House Party, and EMH had been at all 27. She received what she was delighted to call a "one-and-only" quilt, with all the associations of Texas plus the two states of Minnesota-Wisconsin represented. A "This Is Your Life" program was the highlight of one evening session with persons coming from different parts of the United States to participate, and a brochure outlining her 34 years of service was distributed. Much to the delight of those present, EMH was asked to take part in each general session with a "This I Remember" time. She enjoyed it, as did the audience.

Perhaps one of the most meaningful times of the year came during that House Party when Eula Mae had the privilege of introducing her successor, Joy Phillips Fenner, to the House Party. It was a high moment for EMH; she was delighted with her successor.

The One Hundred Days of Prayer, begun on July 28, climaxed on October 5 at First Baptist Church in Austin, when approximately 1,000 Texas WMUers gathered to mark the 100th birthday of the organization in the church where it had begun. The church had occupied a new sanctuary since 1969; hence, at the conclusion of the service, Eula Mae and Mrs. Egge led the group on a four-block pilgrimage to 10th and

Colorado Streets where the original church had stood. Special guests for this historic day were relatives of Fannie Breedlove Davis, the first state president, and members of the Bagby family. (Anne Luther—later Mrs. William Buck Bagby—had been examined for foreign mission service in that church the same day WMU of Texas was organized.) Meanwhile, around the state those who could not attend the Austin event were having associational centennial birthday parties.

At the Annual Meeting in Houston, the spotlight was focused both on Huis Coy Egge who was finishing her tenure as president, and on Eula Mae, about to conclude her lengthy service with Texas WMU. The traditional luncheon honoring the president featured a Mexican motif in tribute to Mrs. Egge's work with the Hispanic people through the years. Pastors and co-workers with whom she had served brought tributes. Her contributions were many, and many-faceted, both on the state and national level. At the time of her retirement in Texas, she had begun serving a five-year term with the North American Baptist Fellowship, having been elected at the WMU, SBC Annual Meeting in St. Louis earlier in the year.

THIS I REMEMBER: At times when I stop and look back, I realize there is no way to measure or evaluate the influence that Eula Mae had on my life.

I remember that she was a motivator, an encourager, a caring friend. But I also remember something else because it impressed me so much. She was a person of deep and sincere humility. She never saw herself personally as someone special.

As she approached retirement, I was asked, as chairman of the Personnel Committee, to visit with her and see if she would consider staying longer. I made an appointment. When the time came, we visited together briefly, then I told her the reason for my visit: the committee wondered if she would consider working a while longer.

She looked at me, and gratitude flooded her face. Gently she explained that it would not be best for Texas WMU—or for her—to remain on the job. Then she added, "I am so grateful that you would want me to stay—and so relieved. I wondered if I had done something wrong!"

She was grateful that "we wanted her." Then I was the one overwhelmed. It was a beautiful form of humility.
    —Gerry Dunkin, President, WMU of Texas, 1988-92

Mauriece Johnston was nominated to serve as state President again, having already served from 1980 to 1984, and was elected. Across the state, some concern had been expressed that a new president and a new Executive Director-Treasurer could make an unduly heavy burden; the Nominating Committee felt led to combine experience with the fresh approach a new worker would bring.

The meeting had many happy times for EMH with many

surprises. It began with the printed program itself. It was white, with an embossed centennial logo. The inside front page had a color picture of Eula Mae with this inscription: "This Centennial program is affectionately dedicated to Eula Mae Henderson, beloved Executive Director-Treasurer of Woman's Missionary Union of Texas, whose FAITH in the women of Texas, HOPE in the missionary cause, and LOVE of the Savior have endeared her to all of us." She knew about the awarding of centennial scrolls to associations and churches who had met centennial goals. Then came more surprises: the public announcement of the Henderson Missions Trust Fund, the fact that she was named Executive Director-Treasurer Emeritus, the unveiling of a large portrait of her to hang in the WMU office, a sterling knife, fork, and ice tea spoon to complete her service, and, at the BGCT Convention, President Carlos McLeod's gift of two dozen yellow roses, plus a Waterford crystal bowl, on behalf of the convention.

Coming home, EMH wrote, "I was surprised and overwhelmed several times. I took an extra suitcase to Houston filled with 'thank you's.' Even so, I ran out and needed more! I shall try to live out my gratitude to Woman's Missionary Union of Texas and to the Lord for all His goodness to me. I say with the Psalmist, 'Lord, with all my heart, I thank you.'" [10]

December of 1980, EMH's last month in office, also brought another of those special times that meant so much to her. Her work with River Ministry had been both enduring and endearing since 1967. Shortly before her retirement, Elmin Howell and the River Ministry team sponsored an appreciation dinner for her. She received tributes, plaques, and gifts. Also, as recorded in *With These Hands*, she "was more than a little surprised by the 'gift' from the agricultural ministries. (It was) Prissy, a Nubian milk goat, (who) 'stole the show.' Every time she was near Miss Henderson, she nibbled the honoree's corsage. The honoree did not know whether to laugh or cry! She was greatly relieved when someone suggested she could return Prissy to the World Hunger Farm and leave her there."[11]

And so 1980 came to an end. Eula Mae Henderson had completed her years of service with Texas WMU, but not her work for missions. That was still an "Unfinished Journey."

MANTLE OF LEADERSHIP PASSES—Smiles on the faces of both Eula Mae and Joy Phillips Fenner (right) reflect the gratitude and happiness that each felt when the mantle of the Executive Director-Treasurer of Texas WMU was passed from one to the other at the end of 1980. Joy had served on Eula Mae's staff, married Charlie Fenner, served with him as a missionary to Japan, then at the invitation of Texas WMU, accepted the position her mentor was vacating. "I couldn't be happier with the selection," Eula Mae said as she presented Joy to the Executive Board.

10

Journey's End . . . and a Lengthening Legacy

"Heaven welcomed home a queen today."

Eula Mae, retired less than a week, was perched on a six-foot ladder in her living room, busily engaged in painting the ceiling. She looked down at Millie Bishop who had just arrived from Plainview and said, "I'm glad to see you, but I can't come down just yet. I promised myself I would work until 5. Have a seat, and I'll be down in just a few minutes." Whereupon she dipped her paint brush in a can that appeared almost empty, smiled warmly at her guest, and resumed her task.

It was, of course, a matter of self-assignment, or perhaps dual-assignment, since she and Erma had decided on how to handle the transition into retirement for both of them. They would begin by painting the inside of their town house, one room at a time.

Erma, who had also retired in December, had moved to Dallas and joined her sister in the town house in Garland they had purchased two years earlier. They worked out a schedule for painting the house, a project that would ease them into retirement. However, that particular schedule left some question as to the meaning of "retirement."

They joined the Mission Service Corps, and opted to work for the Hispanic Baptist Seminary in San Antonio, having been invited to do so by Dan Rivera, then President of the seminary. Hoping to acquire some knowledge of the Spanish language, they signed up for a basic course in the language at the seminary, and moved into the seminary dorm in the spring of 1981 for a brief stay.

All too soon, however, it was time for the Southern Baptist Convention in Los Angeles. Eula Mae was to be recognized as one of the Outstanding Alumni of Southwestern Baptist Theological Seminary at the institution's traditional luncheon. They traveled to California with friends, and the trip proved to be a culinary delight. Eula Mae rode in the back seat with a map in one hand and a guidebook to favorite eating places in the other. As soon as lunch was over, she promptly began working on where to have dinner. The travelers all benefitted from her research.

Returning from the convention with an impressive plaque from Southwestern Seminary in hand, Eula Mae began to ponder a question she had asked herself before. What should she do with the variety of plaques she had received during her years of denominational service? She was grateful for each one, yet she didn't know what to do with them. She couldn't bring herself to display them, yet she wanted them as mementos. She solved the problem by arranging them on the back wall of her bedroom walk-in closet. Thus she could enjoy them, but they weren't on display.

Meanwhile, having been exposed to the Spanish language, the Henderson sisters decided that perhaps language was not a strong point of theirs, but working for the Hispanic Seminary was. At the state convention in November, they worked in the Hispanic Seminary booth, and EMH received a number of invitations to speak, adding to the ones she already had. Some of the requests pertained to weeks of prayer and other special occasions, but many were to tell the story of the seminary.

In June of 1982, another honor came her way. She was named "Texas Baptist Elder Statesman" amid appropriate ceremonies at Independence, Texas. William M. Pinson, Jr., Executive Director of the Baptist General Convention of Texas, had a part on the program along with other denominational leaders. Joy Phillips Fenner brought the message of the day. The plaque awarded her that day was given a place of honor in her collection.

The habit of years was strong. EMH was involved in speaking engagements, keeping up with the Hispanic Seminary, and local church activities. Also, she was planning a short mission trip to the Northeast, and another overseas tour to Africa.

THIS I REMEMBER: Eula Mae's trips had many highlights, and some of them were humorous. This one was—decidedly!

Four of us (Eula Mae, Erma, Dr. Ada Smith, and myself) were on a mission trip to the Northeast, and stopped in a small country church for Sunday morning worship, slipping quietly into the back row. When the time came for the special music, the pastor looked around, and, not seeing the expected musicians, asked if there were any volunteers.

One proud father, whose children had gone to summer camp and learned some new songs, volunteered his two children. They went to the front.

The song had two or three verses, and a chorus, often repeated. That part came in loud and clear: ". . . worms . . . worms . . . worms . . ."

It was decidedly a song about worms. Fine for camp, but for Sunday morning . . . ? Startled, I glanced down the pew at Eula Mae, who was leaning forward to be sure she heard right. Then I saw her lean back and bow her head, struggling for composure. In a moment I felt the pew begin to shake, she was laughing that hard.

The rest of the congregation seemed unperturbed. We swallowed, and tried to match their demeanor. After the service, we spoke briefly with some of the friendly folks and with the pastor. None of them mentioned the music.

We certainly did not. But the memory lingers on!
—Eunice Chambless

Planning for any EMH-led tour began at least eighteen months in advance. The Africa trip was no exception. Molly Houser, who had served in Africa for more than 25 years with her husband, Jim, related how Eula Mae called her early in 1981 to discuss the weather in Africa at specific times, what clothing would be appropriate, and similar matters. The trip was more than a year in the future, but the plans were well under way.

The months intervening passed more quickly than Eula Mae would have wished. In July of 1982, she, Erma, and their group took off on a three-week trek that was to prove more eventful than any had anticipated.

When the group arrived in Nairobi, Kenya, they were met by missionaries Al and Peggy Cummins. Because the travelers had been through areas fomenting with unrest, Al commented, "Welcome to the safest country in Africa!"

This was, as it turned out, just days before a military coup which threw Kenya into an uproar, and temporarily unseated the government. When it happened, the tour group had left Nairobi and stopped at Abermarle for a quick changeover. Unaware of the problem, Eula Mae went into the office to announce their arrival and get instructions. She was gone longer than usual, and returned to say in measured tones, "There has been a military coup, and at present the rebels are in control of the country. We are in no danger, but we will need to wait here until we have permission to go on."

The group filed off the bus, drank coffee, then EMH suggested, "Since it is Sunday morning, I believe we can find a place to have our Sunday morning services." They did so, and shortly after that, were given permission to leave.

Traveling toward Mt. Kenya, the group stopped at the equator to pick up souvenirs at one of the shops dotting the landscape. They were milling around their bus taking pictures when a rebel soldier waving a rifle appeared and ordered them to get back on the bus and to leave. Encouraged by the rifle, they did so.

The balance of the trip to the Mt. Kenya Lodge was uneventful, albeit characterized by a certain amount of inner stress. A few days later, the previous government regained control and the group returned to Nairobi. They were met by Al Cummins who asked with tongue-in-cheek, remembering his welcome, "Well, how's my credibility?"

Portions of the hotel where they had been staying had been strafed and many workers could not get into town, which made for limited service and a vastly curtailed menu. No one was allowed on the streets before sunrise or after sunset. However, the group was safe; the rest was just inconvenience. This was EMH's last overseas trip, her last big project.

Eula Mae continued her regular pace through 1983, but in 1984, the cancer reappeared. Again she underwent treatment and accepted fewer engagements, since her strength was limited. She was able, however, in January 1985, to attend the dedication of the new WMU, SBC building in Birmingham. The occasion was especially meaningful to her as she recalled her relationship with national workers through the years, as well as those times when she and other state leaders had worked together on national projects.

Undoubtedly, she was considered a leader by national WMU. Both Alma Hunt and Carolyn Weatherford (Crumpler), national executive directors with whom she had worked, attested to her leadership abilities and recounted instances in which her contributions made a decided difference. National presidents Marie Mathis, Helen Fling, and Christine (Mrs. A. Harrison) Gregory echoed the refrain. Two other national presidents, Dorothy (Mrs. Richard) Sample and Marjorie (Mrs. Glendon) McCullough, who held office after Eula Mae retired but knew her in other capacities, have written appreciably of both EMH's capabilities and influence on the national level.

Eula Mae's last engagement was a women's retreat for Woodlawn Baptist Church in Garland where her longtime friend, Evelyn Beaird, served as Baptist Women President. EMH had accepted the invitation several months earlier, but her condition took a decided turn for the worse, and her strength was limited. However, she was determined to keep the engagement. The difficulty was solved by Evelyn's arranging for the special guest to limit her activity at the retreat and to remain seated while she spoke.

In April of 1985, at home with Erma in the evening, EMH started to walk across the room and collapsed on the floor, her strength drained and her legs unable to hold her up. From that point on, she was bedridden.

Her visitors during the ensuing months were varied, and as many as her strength permitted. Her demeanor remained outwardly calm and composed, at times even radiant. However, she was deeply concerned about the controversy in the Southern Baptist Convention, as exemplified by one visit from Alma Hunt and Helen Fling. They came to see her just prior to the SBC meeting in Dallas in the summer of 1985. The three longtime friends chatted amiably and before their departure, Helen said, "Eula Mae, I want Alma to lead us in prayer for you before we leave." Very quickly, Eula Mae shook her head and replied, "No, I'm all right. But my convention isn't. Please, Alma, pray for the Southern Baptist Convention." And Alma did.[1]

By November it became evident that the end would not be long in coming. It wasn't. The first few days of December, she appeared to be slipping in and out of a coma. Close friends began to take turns staying with Eula Mae and Erma during the night. In the early hours of December 5, 1985, Eula Mae's breathing changed, and then, at 5:05 A.M., stopped altogether. Erma, Evelyn Beaird, and Millie Bishop were at her bedside.

Joy and Charlie Fenner came over immediately. Later in the morning, the Baptist Building in Dallas and national WMU in Birmingham were notified. The WMU office activated a plan to immediately inform the Executive Board. Bob Dixon, Executive Director of Texas Baptist Men, expressed the feelings of many when he said, "Heaven welcomed home a queen today."

In typical EMH fashion, Eula Mae had worked out her memorial service. It was held in Embree Hall at First Baptist Church in Dallas, with her pastor, W.A. Criswell, presiding. Charles McLaughlin, Director of the BGCT State Missions Commission, brought the message; Millie Bishop, then President of Woman's Missionary Union of Texas, delivered the eulogy; Bob Dixon prayed; and Martha Brannan, soloist at numerous state and national Baptist meetings, sang. The focus, at Eula Mae's request, was on missions. The entire service was "vintage Eula Mae."

In retrospect, what were Eula Mae's leadership qualities? What were her contributions?

Many of those who spoke of her as a leader, both in her long tenure at Texas WMU and in the brief years that followed, invariably stressed several of the same qualities. The composite of these sketch her leadership profile.

She demonstrated an unswerving level of commitment to prayer and Bible study; this was foundational to all she did. That same commitment was seen in her devotion to and enthusiasm for her work; it was contagious. She led by example. She was clear-headed, decisive, strong—yet friendly and affirming. In fact, she was consistently an encourager, both with her staff and with hosts of volunteers through the years. In the process, she took risks with inexperienced people and helped them grow. Several persons (including Wilma Reed, Minette Drumwright, Gerry Dunkin, Debra Hochgraber, and others) voiced the same thought, "She believed I could do things that I myself didn't think I could. I surprised myself!" She maintained a positive attitude both toward the task ahead and those involved. Several indicated that, "She didn't know the meaning of negative!"

Dollie Culp, who served as administrative assistant in the state WMU office until 1972, remembered the drive from Waco back to Dallas when the WMU House Party was over. "Eula Mae would be on top of the world, literally glowing. And she spoke happily of every highlight of the meeting—the good things—she never mentioned the negatives." Yes, she knew about them, but seemingly she saved them for her "How can we do this better" sessions.[2]

Eula Mae was a woman of vision. Frances Stroope, who followed Dollie in the administrative assistant position, referred to Eula Mae as a transformational leader. "She challenged us to think in new ways, to discover new approaches to our missions task. Her vision, personal values, and commitment inspired me to put forth my best efforts."[3]

Other missions leaders with whom she worked in the BGCT structure also attested to her visionary capabilities. Charles McLaughlin, Charles Lee Williamson, and Elmin Howell have all pointed to watershed times when "Eula Mae stood her ground; it made a big difference in what happened then, and in the years that followed. Her looking ahead and holding the line altered the course of missions programs and missions giving."

She maintained an ongoing personal interest in people, remembering their names, where they lived, and often something about their families. Lynette Adam and June Castle spoke of occasions when they "felt taller because she remembered the personal things." Mary Lou Serratt and Laura Harris—among others—referred to her thoughtfulness, her sense of humor, her ability to motivate.

And yet . . . and yet . . .

Assuredly, Eula Mae did not walk on water, as those who knew her best could attest. She was very much human, and like other human beings, she had her faults. Perhaps it was ironic that some of her bedrock commitments at times operated against her. For instance, the lodestar of her life was missions and missions education. Therefore, the salary she made and the amount of time needed to get the job done were unimportant to her. The problem came in that when she felt she did not need a salary increase, that automatically limited the raises to her staff.

Also, her commitment to presenting WMU in the best light sometimes ran into generational gaps in the latter years of her tenure. On one occasion, she was the last director in the Baptist Building to permit her staff to wear pantsuits to work. The day after she gave permission to do so, she was out of town. The three staffers who wore pantsuits that day were accused of "When the boss is away, the minions will play!"

She seemed to believe that she should work out her own problems and not bother others with them—she was a very private person. This could sometimes work against her. She felt strongly that if staffers had problems between them, she should respect their right to work out the difficulty themselves. Being optimistic by nature, she believed they would. So she was reluctant to step in. She had no problem in standing up for a conviction, an ideal, a program she believed in, but she tended to step back from negative situations involving personalities.

Perhaps her most difficult time as a state leader came in the last few years of her tenure when—in a matter of several months—her age-level workers left for other positions. True, such work had often proved to be a stepping stone to something else, yet the turnover caused her deep concerns in several areas, principally about herself as a leader and her own decision-making process. New workers were already coming, but in the meantime, she was deeply disturbed. After several months of prayer, committee consultation, and soul-searching, she went forward one Sunday night in her church and rededicated her life, offering no explanation to her pastor, but saying simply, "This is something I need to do."

Eula Mae moved forward. If the problem was with her, she wanted to face it, to change, to put down a period, and to move on. In essence, this is what she did.

Certainly a tribute to her leadership has been seen in the number of her former staffers who have continued in the work of missions education, and assumed positions on the state and national levels: Joy Fenner, Executive Director-Treasurer of WMU of Texas; Mary Jane Nethery, who became Executive Director of Tennessee WMU, and was succeeded in that position by Katharine Bryan; Barbara Curnutt, who became Executive Director of Florida WMU; Elaine Dickson, Sheryl

Churchill, Marsha Spradlin, and Nell Carter Branum, all of whom have been associated with national WMU; and Amelia (Millie) Bishop, who became President of Texas WMU. Evelyn Tully was never on the Texas staff, but she grew up surrounded by Texas WMU, and became Executive Director of Illinois WMU. Eula Mae claimed her as "one of ours," and Evelyn referred to EMH as her role model.

THIS I REMEMBER: *I can't remember when I didn't know who Eula Mae Henderson was. Surely the whole world knows Miss Henderson!*

My mother had the same feeling. I recall that once in Virginia, mother brought up Eula Mae's name in connection with a prayer request, and was totally surprised to learn that the Virginia women did not know her!

We, of course, did. In fact, she was an important person in our lives even before we (my husband, Bill, and myself) went to the mission field. On one of our first furloughs, she graciously invited us to take part in the Texas WMU Annual Meeting—Bill to lead the music, and I to play the piano. It was a choice time. Eula Mae had a special love for missionaries, and that love was returned.

Then, it was Texas WMU who commissioned Bill and Dick Anthony to write "Harvest" for the 1977 Week of Prayer for State Missions in Texas, and it was premiered at House Party that year. That, also, was special.

In missions education, Eula Mae was a strong leader, a pivotal leader. Along with that, she was a caring and generous friend.

Bill has been quoted as saying, "I must tell you that there are two other women in my life other than my wife—and I have told her this also! One is Alma Hunt, and one is Eula Mae Henderson."

How thankful we both are that this has been true.
—Dellanna O'Brien

In summary, Eula Mae exemplified many of the characteristics that others look for in a Christian leader. Those who came under her influence felt this; they sensed her authenticity. They came to love her for who she was and what she represented. They followed her because she led by example. Many ranked her as "one of the most influential persons in my life."

And that ongoing influence is what constitutes, in part, her lengthening legacy.

Paralleling this, and undoubtedly springing from it, is another part of her legacy: her contributions to the work of missions and missions education.

Those who have sought to evaluate the Henderson years have often pointed to the high standard she set in the larger sense of programming, meaning "that which is done during the WMU year." Her strong emphasis on sustained training for all levels—church, associational, district (in the early years) and state—paid rich dividends. Such an emphasis served not only to educate the women, but also had two corollary benefits: it brought vitality to missions education and helped, in many instances, to integrate WMU as a basic program. Eula Mae believed that each of the basic programs of the local church had a distinctive contribution to make, and she promoted this concept. Her own work for thirty years in a Junior Sunday School department of her church demonstrated her conviction.

In the training area, after districts were abolished in Texas in the early 1960s, Eula Mae began to feel after a period of time that "We lost something when we lost the district level. We need more connection between the state office and the associations." Hence in the late 1970s the WMU began the Coordinator program, dividing the state into groupings of associations, with a volunteer serving as coordinator in each area. This was a seed idea that was eventually developed into an effective Associational Leadership Team Equipper program.

Her approach to total programming involved prayer, planning, and promotion. State-level events such as annual meetings or house parties—now TLC (Texas Leadership

Conference)—were characterized by strong missionary speakers, excellent music, and dramatic presentations when the facilities permitted. No details were left to chance, and timing was of the essence. With a bit of a smile, Eula Mae would say to participants, "Now please don't waste your time talking about the fact that you wish you had more time." She also believed that since state workshops were indeed work, fellowship should also be programmed in. "It makes it fun to come," she would say. It worked. This was an era when women's schedules and lifestyles permitted more flexibility.

EMH strengthened the relationship of WMU with pastors in Texas and with the Baptist General Convention of Texas. Helen Fling described EMH's relationship with pastors by saying, "Eula Mae had a singular regard for the pastor's role in developing a missionary church. She wrote countless personal letters to pastors and their people, commending them for their support of the Cooperative Program, seasons of prayer offerings, unusual local ministries, or missions experiences. She seemed to find special satisfaction in helping young pastors nurture missions effectively, and rejoiced as many Texas pastors and their wives volunteered for overseas missions or work in our pioneer areas."[4]

William M. Pinson, Jr., who had worked with Eula Mae prior to his coming to the executive position, commented on her relationship with the state convention. "She strengthened the ties between us, and helped Texas Baptists to feel both positive and excited about missions. She worked at it from her early days in leadership."[5]

Seemingly she did, from the time she was made a part of "the Baptist Building team" by J. Howard Williams, then Executive Secretary. Eula Mae was both pleased and appreciative, and made it a policy to support other areas of work. At the same time, other directors likewise supported WMU, recognizing the auxiliary relationship, but stressing the team approach to missions. Obviously there were times when the leadership team had differences of opinion, but the feeling of partnership prevailed. This type of relationship, ongoing over a period of years, helped to make the Mary Hill Davis Offering for State Missions an integral part of Texas Baptist life. In the same area, Eula Mae had stood with Marie Mathis in the 1950s in making the Lottie Moon and Annie Armstrong Offerings churchwide, a significant contribution.

In summary, she was strong in planning a balanced program for WMU involving training and special events; she helped to build a strong relationship with Texas Baptist pastors and with the Baptist General Convention of Texas and its leadership; she helped to make the Lottie Moon and Annie Armstrong Offerings churchwide; and she worked to make the Mary Hill Davis Offering an integral part of Texas Baptist life. Her conviction about missions monies never wavered. Additionally, credit must be given for her role in the beginning and early years of the River Ministry, her work with Hispanics—including the Latin American scholarships—and her assistance in the work in Minnesota-Wisconsin.

All in all, Eula Mae was a woman who lived out her convictions. And Texas Baptists—and the world—have been blessed by it.

Mary Valerio phrased it this way: "She was totally believable—she walked the talk."[6]

Carolyn Weatherford (Crumpler) said, "She had the respect of her peers and of her people because she had earned it. She was a strong and effective leader."[7]

Nell Carter (Branum) said, "She modeled so many of the qualities we look for in leadership, and became a legend because others made her one."[8]

Presnall Wood, then editor of *The Baptist Standard,* wrote, "Texas Baptists have always been missions-minded, but Eula Mae Henderson has played a large part in seeing 'how far we can get.' She will be remembered as one of Texas Baptists' most gracious leaders."[9]

They were right.

"Lord, in Thy name we face tomorrow's needs
Content to follow where Thy Spirit leads
As others served Thee long and faithfully
So may we bring the best we have to Thee."[10]

Notes

In June, 1995, a request for information entitled "Questionnaire: Eula Mae Henderson" was sent to her friends and co-workers. The responses were quite similar in many instances, in which case they formed a composite and were not footnoted. In individual instances, a footnote was used.

Material used in "This I Remember" throughout the book was supplied by the person named in each recollection, and taken from responses to the Henderson questionnaire and from letters to Amelia Bishop.

Chapter One
1. Interview with Erma Henderson Barnett, Garland, Texas, 15 June, 1995.
2. Ibid.
3. Eula Mae Henderson, Oral History Memoir, Texas Collection, Baylor University, p. 3.
4. Ibid., p. 9-10.
5. Ibid., p. 8.
6. Ibid., pp. 16-18.
7. Ibid., p. 14.

Chapter Two
1. Eula Mae Henderson, Oral History Memoir, p. 25.
2. Oleta Snell, response to Henderson Questionnaire, August 1995.
3. Frances Osborne, response to Henderson Questionnaire, August 1995.
4. Amelia Bishop, personal recollection incorporated into body of material.
5. Ibid.
6. Floyce Moon, response to Henderson Questionnaire, August 1995.
7. Eddie Jo Connell (Bazor), response to Henderson Questionnaire, September 1995.
8. Eula Mae Henderson, Oral History Memoir, pp.29-30.
9. Floyce Moon, response to Henderson Questionnaire, August 1995.

Chapter Three
   1. Proceedings of Annual Meeting of Woman's Missionary Union of Texas, 1947.
   2. Eula Mae Henderson, Oral History Memoir, p. 38.
   3. Roberta Turner Patterson, *Candle by Night* (Dallas, Texas: Woman's Missionary Union of Texas, 1955), p. 122.
   4. Inez Boyle Hunt, *Century One: A Pilgrimage of Faith* (Dallas, Texas, Woman's Missionary Union of Texas, 1979), p. 51.
   5. Ibid.
   6. Nobie McGill, response to Henderson Questionnaire, September 1995.
   7. Jimmy Allen, response to Henderson Questionnaire, September 1995.
   8. Minutes of Executive Board, Woman's Missionary Union of Texas, September 1949.
   9. Ibid.
   10. Proceedings of Annual Meeting of Woman's Missionary Union of Texas, November 1950.

Chapter Four
   1. Alma Hunt, letter to Amelia Bishop, January, 1996.
   2. Minutes of Executive Board of Woman's Missionary Union of Texas, September 1951.
   3. Eula Mae Henderson, Oral History Memoir, p. 42.
   4. Ibid., p. 43.
   5. Ibid., pp. 43-44.
   6. Inez Boyle Hunt, *Century One: A Pilgrimage of Faith*, p. 55.
   7. Ibid., p. 56.
   8. Ibid., p. 55.
   9. Minutes of Executive Board, Woman's Missionary Union of Texas, September 1953.
   10. Amelia Bishop, personal recollection incorporated into body of material.
   11. Ibid.
   12. Ibid.
   13. Ibid.

Chapter Five
   1. Minutes of Executive Board, Woman's Missionary Union of Texas, March 1955.
   2. Louise Yelvington Denham, personal letter to Amelia Bishop, September 1997.
   3. Catherine B. Allen, *A Century to Celebrate* (Birmingham, Alabama, Woman's Missionary Union, Auxiliary to Southern Baptist Convention, 1987), p. 162.
   4. Eula Mae Henderson, Oral History Memoir, p. 77.
   5. Joshua Grijalva, *A History of Mexican Baptists in Texas* (Dallas, Texas: Office of Language Missions in cooperation with the Mexican Baptist Convention of Texas, 1982), p. 32.

6. Ibid., pp. 115-121.
7. Amelia Bishop and Charles McLaughlin, "Other Texas Baptist Entities," *Baptists: History, Distinctives, Relationships*, ed. E. Eugene Greer, Jr. (Dallas, Texas: Baptist General Convention of Texas, Church Services Division, 1996), p. 121.
8. Inez Boyle Hunt, *Century One: A Pilgrimage of Faith*, p. 63.
9. Catherine B. Allen, *A Century to Celebrate*, p. 436.
10. Inez Boyle Hunt, *Century One: A Pilgrimage of Faith*, p. 64.

Chapter Six
1. Eula Mae Henderson, letter to Executive Board, Woman's Missionary Union of Texas, 25 April 1962.
2. Eula Mae Henderson, letter to Executive Board, 8 June 1962.
3. Eula Mae Henderson, letter to Executive Board, 5 July 1962.
4. Ibid.
5. Eula Mae Henderson, letter to Executive Board, 15 October 1962.
6. Proceedings of Annual Meeting of Woman's Missionary Union of Texas, 11-12 November 1963.
7. Dollie Culp, response to Henderson Questionnaire, October 1995.
8. Leila Black, letter to Executive Board, Woman's Missionary Union of Texas, 7 December 1963.
9. Ophelia Humphrey, Oral History Memoir (Interview Two, draft copy) Texas Collection, Baylor University, p. 6.
10. Proceedings of Annual Meeting of Woman's Missionary Union of Texas, 1964. (Attachment to minutes from Woman's Missionary Union, Corpus Christi Baptist Association.)
11. Katharine Bryan, response to Henderson Questionnaire, October 1995.
12. Joy Fenner, personal letter to Amelia Bishop, August 1995.
13. Ibid.

Chapter Seven
1. Wilma K. Reed and Elmin Howell, Jr., *With These Hands* (Dallas, Texas: River Ministry Section, Baptist General Convention of Texas, 1982), p. 32. Since a second edition of *With These Hands* came out in 1992, the 1982 book is sometimes referred to as Vol. I.
2. Ophelia Humphrey, Oral History Memoir (Interview Two, draft copy) p. 14.
3. Minutes of State Missions Commission, Baptist General Convention of Texas, 17 February 1967.
4. Wilma Reed, Ken Camp, and Elmin Howell, Jr., *With These Hands*, Vol. II (Dallas, Texas: River Ministry Section, Baptist General Convention of Texas, 1992), p. 11.
5. Wilma Reed and Elmin Howell, Jr., *With These Hands*, Vol. I, p. 10.
6. Eula Mae Henderson, Oral History Memoir, p. 57.
7. Proceedings of Annual Meeting, Woman's Missionary Union of Texas, 1967.
8. Ibid.

9. Inez Boyle Hunt, *Century One: A Pilgrimage of Faith*, p. 77.
10. Ibid., p. 78.
11. Lynn Yarbrough, letter to Amelia Bishop, August 1995.
12. Gerry Dunkin, response to Henderson Questionnaire, October 1995.
13. Linda Lyle, letter to Amelia Bishop, November 1995.
14. Claudia Jones Swain, response to Henderson Questionnaire, September 1995.
15. Inez Boyle Hunt, *Century One: A pilgrimage of Faith*, pp. 78-79.
16. Joy Pitts, response to Henderson Questionnaire, September 1995.

Chapter Eight
1. Inez Boyle Hunt, Oral History Memoirs, Texas Collection, Baylor University, p. 24.
2. Catherine B. Allen, *A Century to Celebrate*, p. 111-112, 439.
3. Eula Mae Henderson, Oral Memoir, pp. 52-53.
4. Inez Boyle Hunt, *Century One: A Pilgrimage of Faith*, p. 85.
5. Sheryl Churchill, response to Henderson Questionnaire, August 1995.
6. Minutes of Executive Board, Woman's Missionary Union of Texas, March 1971.
7. Eula Mae Henderson, letter to Executive Board, Woman's Missionary Union of Texas, 3 May 1972.
8. Eula Mae Henderson, letter to Executive Board, 17 May 1972.
9. Eula Mae Henderson, letter to Executive Board, 31 January 1972.
10. Eula Mae Henderson, letter to Executive Board, 7 February 1972.
11. Eula Mae Henderson, letter to Executive Board, 31 January 1972.
12. Eula Mae Henderson, letter to Executive Board, 12 June 1972.
13. Evelyn Beaird, letter to Amelia Bishop, February 1996.
14. Minutes of Executive Board, October 1972.
15. Mauriece Johnston, Oral History Memoir (Interview Three, draft copy), Texas Collection, Baylor University, pp. 36-37.
16. Claudia Jones Swain, letter to Amelia Bishop, September 1995.
17. Inez Boyle Hunt, *Century One: A Pilgrimage of Faith*, p. 91.

Chapter Nine
1. Eula Mae Henderson, letter to Executive Board, 17 February 1977.
2. Eula Mae Henderson, letter to Executive Board, 18 January 1978.
3. Minutes of Executive Board, March 15 1978. (Henderson speech appended.)
4. Eula Mae Henderson, letter to Executive Board, 9 June 1978.
5. Eula Mae Henderson, letter to Executive Board, 14 September 1978.
6. Inez Boyle Hunt, *Century One: A Pilgrimage of Faith*, p. 98.
7. Eula Mae Henderson, letter to Executive Board, 15 November 1978.
8. Eula Mae Henderson, letter to Executive Board, 24 April 1979.

9. Millie Kohn, response to Henderson Questionnaire, September 1995.
10. Eula Mae Henderson, letter to Executive Board, 4 November 1980.
11. Wilma K. Reed and Elmin Howell, Jr., *With These Hands*, Vol. I, p. 39.

Chapter Ten
1. Alma Hunt, letter to Amelia Bishop, January 1996.
2. Dollie Culp, response to Henderson Questionnaire, September 1995.
3. Frances Stroope, letter to Amelia Bishop, September 1995.
4. Helen Fling, letter to Amelia Bishop, January 1996.
5. William M. Pinson, Jr., response to Henderson Questionnaire, August 1995.
6. Mary Valerio, response to Henderson Questionnaire, September 1995.
7. Carolyn Weatherford Crumpler, response to Henderson Questionnaire, September 1995.
8. Nell Carter Branum, letter to Amelia Bishop, September 1995.
9. Presnall Wood, *The Baptist Standard*, 15 October 1980.
10. Sybil Leonard Armes, Texas WMU Centennial Song, 1980.

Bibliography

Published Materials:

Allen, Catherine B. *A Century to Celebrate*. Birmingham, Alabama: Woman's Missionary Union, Auxiliary to Southern Baptist Convention, 1987.

Bishop, Amelia, and McLaughlin, Charles. "Other Texas Baptist Entities," *Baptists: History, Distinctives, Relationships*. Edited by E. Eugene Greer, Jr. Dallas, Texas: Church Services Division, Baptist General Convention of Texas, 1996.

Grijalva, Joshua. *A History of Mexican Baptists in Texas*. Dallas, Texas: Office of Language Missions, Baptist General Convention of Texas, in cooperation with Mexican Baptist Convention of Texas, 1982.

Hunt, Inez Boyle. *Century One: A Pilgrimage of Faith*. Dallas, Texas: Woman's Missionary Union of Texas, 1979.

Patterson, Roberta Turner. *Candle by Night*. Dallas, Texas: Woman's Missionary Union of Texas, 1955.

Wood, Presnall, editorial, *The Baptist Standard* (Dallas, Texas), 15 October 1980.

Other Sources:

Baptist General Convention of Texas. State Missions Commission, Minutes of 17 February 1967.

Barnett, Erma Henderson. Garland, Texas. Interview, 15 June 1995.

Egge, Huis Coy. Oral Memoirs, Texas Collection, Baylor University, Waco, Texas.

Henderson, Eula Mae. Letters (Memos) to Executive Board, Woman's Missionary Union of Texas. 1962-1980.

_____. Oral Memoirs, Texas Collection, Baylor University, Waco, Texas.

Humphrey, Ophelia. Oral Memoirs (Draft Copy), Texas Collection, Baylor University, Waco, Texas.

Hunt, Inez Boyle. Oral Memoirs, Texas Collection, Baylor University, Waco, Texas.

Johnston, Mauriece. Oral Memoirs (Draft Copy), Texas Collection, Baylor University, Waco, Texas.

Responses to Eula Mae Henderson Questionnaire/Personal letters. Woman's Missionary Union Archives, Texas Baptist Historical Collection, Dallas, Texas.

Woman's Missionary Union of Texas. Dallas, Texas. Executive Board Minutes, 1946-1980.

_____. Dallas, Texas. Proceedings of Annual Meeting, 1946-1980.